Get a Grip On the Future Without Losing Your Hold On the Past explores the bewildering complexity of life today and the responses it demands of us. Every area of our lives will be touched over the next two decades by intense social change.

Technology is leading us into cyberspace. Books may become historic relics. Postmodernism is eroding the basic idea of truth. The political world oscillates between imperialism and tribalism. Spiritual hunger is growing – but new generations reject Christian answers.

How do we gain access to the new cultural landscape? How do we develop the personal and social resources to undergird our future journey? How can we carry with us the very best of past experience? Culture demands that we *re-route*; survival demands that we *re-root*.

No Christian leader can avoid these issues. If you want to understand how new generations are receiving – or rejecting – the gospel, then this book is essential reading. Unless Christians engage with this process, they are in danger of being left behind, irrelevant and forgotten.

DO YOU NEED A SPEAKER?

Many Monarch authors, including the author of this book, are willing to come and speak to groups of all sizes. To obtain a current list of authors and topics please write to: Monarch Books, Concorde House, Grenville Place, Mill Hill, London NW7 3SA.

To Colin – the chairman of Chairmen! a billion blessings. £2

Get a Grip
On the Future
Without Losing Your Hold
On the Past

GERARD KELLY

MONARCH
BOOKS

First published by Monarch Books 1999

ISBN 1 85424 430 2

British Library Cataloguing Data
A catalogue record for this book is available
from the British Library.

Designed and produced for the publishers by
Bookprint Creative Services
P.O. Box 827, BN21 3YJ, England.
Printed in Great Britain.

Dedication

To Joseph, Aaron, Anna and Jacob,
ambassadors of the millennial generation

CONTENTS

ACKNOWLEDGEMENTS

If it takes a village to raise a child, it takes a city to write a book. There are literally hundreds of people whose friendships, conversations, ideas and inspiration have played a part in shaping this project. If you are one of those who in recent months has been pinned in a corner and forced to talk about the future, thank you!

Special thanks are due to those who helped to bring the book to birth: Chrissie Kelly; Tony Collins at Monarch; Ben Wickham for help with surfing; Johnny Crawford for photography; Tom Sine for his foreword and other encouragements; Duncan Banks for working with me on the original 'five posts' seminar; Jane Kelly for the regular supply of intriguing and inspiring books; the members of the Cyberpub for world-class conversation; the members of café.net for support, encouragement and prayer; our church family at Chawn Hill. And at Spring Harvest: Jim Partridge, Alan Johnson, members of the Leadership Team and of the Youth and Rage Development and Planning Teams.

This being the digital age, there's no one to thank for the typing.

FOREWORD

As we race into the third millennium, one thing is clear: we are living in a world that's changing at break-neck speed. However, I am constantly frustrated by how few Christian authors try to make sense of that change. We leave the analysis to secular futurists, policy analysts and demographers. As a consequence, most Christian literature seems to be based on the unspoken assumption that we are frozen in a time warp and that the future will simply be an extension of the present.

Gerard Kelly's provocative book, *Get a Grip On the Future Without Losing Your Hold On the Past* is a welcome exception. Kelly takes us on a trip to the infamous Spaghetti Junction and uses this confusing maze of roadways as a metaphor for our common future.

Kelly takes us on a whirlwind tour of a post-modern future, and the new, uncharted world of 'Cyberia'. He argues that we are undergoing a fundamental social transformation that will decisively alter the early decades of the 21st century. Two 'Hinge Generations', X and Y, are the edge of this, leading us all into a post-literate future that isn't 'a single drink, but a cocktail, the taste of instant communication blending with the potency of the moving image, laced with the spice of interaction'.

Then there is Kelly's brilliant analysis of the landscape of tomorrow's rapidly changing world. For the past thirty years I have been struggling to make sense of this landscape. I repeatedly found this book offering fresh understandings of societal change, and insights that I had never come across in any other literature on the future. More than this, Kelly helps us immediately to grasp the implications for our lives and churches – and the creative ways in which we can respond.

Kelly describes how people of faith will need to 're-imagineer the Church' to serve God in a very different world. He urges all generations to be more open to new expressions of faith that resonate with post-modern culture rather than remain locked into the modernity model as though we had some obligation to conform.

Says Kelly, 'Unless young people are allowed to take hold of faith for themselves – to test its durability; to explore its boundaries; to deconstruct and reconstruct its style; to re-root it in the soil of their own lives, they will neither embrace nor uphold Christianity in the culture of the coming century.' We must begin by supporting and encouraging 'hinge leaders' who devote their lives to the changing task of re-rooting faith in Jesus Christ in a new soil.

This book is a must for those who want to 're-imagineer' their lives, congregations and communities in a way that gives fresh expression to the gospel of Jesus Christ in a new land. Here's an opportunity for all of us to open our lives not merely to a new future, but to the surprising work of the Holy Spirit who leads all of us into uncharted territory.

Tom Sine

INTRODUCTION

The future is too important to be left to chance.
Charles Handy[1]

Spaghetti and Orange Crush

A few kilometres north of my home in the West Midlands stands one of the most enduring monuments to the great British age of road-building. 26,000 tonnes of steel, 250,000 tonnes of concrete, 300,000 tonnes of earth and £8.2 million in the making, it operates on 6 levels and brings together 18 route options. It bears the official title of junction 6 of the M6, but within days of its opening had earned the name by which it is now universally known: Spaghetti Junction. The most complex traffic interchange in the UK, Spaghetti Junction is a Medusa of the motorway, throwing a shadow of greyness over the small community of Gravely Hill. By reputation, it is one of the easiest places in England to get lost.

Spaghetti's American cousin is the 5/22/57 interchange in Orange County, California, known to all as Orange Crush Junction. This asphalt panic-attack rises to a mere 2 levels, but all the same manages to knot together 34 route options, with a total of 66 lanes of traffic. Each day, Orange Crush Junction contributes to the success or failure of some 690,000 separate journeys. Similar junctions could be identified in every nation of the developed world. Wherever high-volume, high-speed traffic management is needed there will be the twisting form of the interchange—a writhing snake-pit of cars and concrete which increases in equal measure both traffic capacity and driver stress. The motorway interchange is an abiding symbol of our age.

This book is a response to the existence of just such an interchange. Complex, threatening, unprecedented in its scale, it is just as real as Spaghetti and Orange Crush—but it exists in our cultural rather than our physical geography. As our century closes its eyes for the last time and a new century is born, movements of significant change are surfacing in unconnected areas of our lives, like multi-lane highways converging around us. Gathering pace and complexity, disparate changes compound one another to add up to a corporate change of life, an interchange in the traffic of society. Change is not happening on one level, but simultaneously on many. Diverse fields of enquiry are finding unexpected connections, and spinning off in radical, new directions. Like drivers in the approach to Spaghetti Junction, we see the signs of change flash by with increasing frequency. We are aware of options offered, of choices demanded, of life-changing decisions ahead. Choose your route or the road will choose it for you. We are caught up in the knots of a 'culture junction'.

Get a Grip on the Future is an exploration of this historic interchange, which will demand of us both rerouting and re*rooting*. Rerouting because in the coming two decades every area of our lives will be touched by intense social change, forcing upon us a choice of road. Rerooting because beyond the interchange we will need to find access, in a new cultural landscape, to resources deep enough and rich enough to fund our future journey. To embrace the future with no regard for the past is to throw away centuries of learning and development—and to risk making again the mistakes which history has tried so hard to teach us. Our best course, rather, is to carry with us—into the future—the very best of past experience. To be rooted in something deeper than the surface currents of change. The challenge before us is to embrace all that the future offers without losing our hold on the riches of the past. If the culture junction demands that we reroute, survival, at the same time, demands that we reroot.

Our exploration of the culture junction will fall into three distinct parts.

Part 1, Root Change, introduces the theme of social transformation and argues that the changes we face, growing faster, wider and deeper by the day, add up to a broad cultural shift— a societal 'change of life'. We will set out the unique situation of two generations. Generation X is the last generation to become adult in the twentieth century, just as the Millennial Generation will be the first young adults of the twenty-first. Together these are the junction generations, those who are leading us into our culture's interchange and those who will lead us out of it. The question of the future shape of culture is essentially a question of these two generations.

Part 2, Root Causes, will examine five of the currents of change set to shape the first two decades of the new century: the 'five posts' of Generation X and beyond. Each taking a different perspective or emphasis, the five posts together offer a framework through which to explore the horizons of the future. The five posts framework describes the emerging culture in which the junction generations will live out their adult years, a culture marked by:

- **Post-industrial technology:** Remoulding society and transforming our lives through the shift from machine technology to information processing.
- **Post-literate communication:** Shifting the Western knowledge-base, learning styles and methods of interaction from those founded on the authority of printed text to those of image and hyper-text.
- **Post-modern philosophy:** Undergirding social change with a shift in popular worldview from the certainties of the Enlightenment to a new adventure of ambiguity, uncertainty and diversity.
- **Post-imperial politics:** The new global context, shifting from the old order of political empires, colonies and mono-cultural rule to the new paradox of globalisation and fragmentation—the fast-growing commercial empires of McWorld in the competitive multiplicity of the planetary market-place.
- **Post-Christian spirituality:** Moving popular piety on from the orthodoxy of Christian and other established faiths to the plurality of individualised, experiential faith expressions.[2]

In each of these five areas, we will explore the implications of rerouting—the choices and changes offered to us, and of rerooting—the prospects for Generation X and the Millennials.

Part 3, Root Growth, will draw together these many threads to offer resources for the management of change. How can individuals, families and communities embrace, manage and survive the process of change? We will look in particular at:

- **Rebirth or retrenchment?** How well do we deal with change, individually and corporately? Can we get from where we are to where we will be without drowning?
- **Remote controllers or resourceful friends?** What kind of leaders will the new environment call for?

The notes offered at the ends of chapters contain both publication details and, where available, Internet addresses. It will be clear even at a glance that certain books and web sites crop up very frequently. If you want to explore further the themes of this book, these titles and references offer proven entry-points—I encourage you to use them to the full. If you have comments or questions on the content of *Get a Grip,* I am very happy to receive them. You can e-mail me direct at getagrip@cafe.surfaid.org, or visit the book's web page at http://www.users.surfaid.org/~cafe/getagrip.

Before we set out on the journey we will share, there are three assumptions I have made which are better spelt out now than stumbled over later.

1. That faith matters

As a practising Christian, I write from a perspective informed by the traditions and discoveries of that faith. As an Evangelical, I have lived for twenty-five years in that section of the Christian community which while not the largest group probably makes the most noise. It is inevitable that my own exploration of cultural change will tend towards seeking out the implications for the Christian Church. I am naturally concerned for the future of my own faith community.

However, this is not a journey on which only those of that community are invited. I hope that this book will be of use to many people whose interests are not exhausted by concern for the Church: the parents of children who show all the signs of having been born on another planet; business-people and employers steering small and large organisations through the whitewater rapids of corporate change; ordinary people battling the daily dilemmas and choices of a culture dizzy with transition. I do not apologise for mentioning the Church so often, but I do hope that those for whom this is unfamiliar ground will be able to benefit all the same—to distinguish principle from application and apply it elsewhere. If this book doesn't produce some pointers for the future of the Church, then I will have failed—but equally, it ought to throw up a few other ideas along the way.

2. That change demands a response

There is a school of thought which holds that the Church, rooted as it is in centuries-old tradition, needn't concern itself with minor external diversions such as social transformation. Even if a case can be made for the existence of a cultural interchange somewhere between now and the near future, there is no implication that anything need be done about it. Businesses need to change. Schools must follow suit. But the Church exists on a higher plane where such imperatives don't apply. Individuals who crave the same immunity need only to huddle under the benevolent umbrella of the unchanging Church—to cling like Quasimodo to the altar and cry 'sanctuary'. I do not hold this view. I believe that the Church *must* change. The Church is not trend-driven—it is God's family and lives by other rules—but it is also a cultural and social institution, rooted in a given place and time. If we have any concern for the rising generations, and for those who will follow them, we must look with urgency to the future shape of our

Church. To resist change is to remain relevant to a world that no longer exists. Tom Sine's much-quoted warning in *Wild Hope* is worth repeating here.

> Every denomination and religious organisation I have worked with does long-range planning. Ironically, they do long-range planning as though the future will simply be an extension of the present. As a result, we are chronically surprised by change. In the future, we can no longer afford this luxury.[3]

3. That fear is natural

The third assumption necessary for this journey is that it's OK to be afraid. Motorway driving is never more stressful than in the negotiating of a major interchange. Likewise the culture junction offers us a speeding blur of choices, demanding that we make them fast. Around us others are tackling change in their own way: some bursting ahead with confidence, swapping lanes and making turns like they were born to it; others crawling in the slow lane in a blind panic; others still pulling over, or reversing back down a slip road to be shot of the whole performance. Away in the distance we catch sight of those who have made their choices and sped on. Are they half way home, or hopelessly lost? Should we follow them or plough a different course? As I have discussed cultural change with individuals and groups in recent years, I have met many who are caught in this fear, and genuinely unsure of where to turn. Change brings with it uncertainty, apprehension and sometimes panic. But it can be the very stimulus we need to reach new heights of creativity, opening up new avenues to explore. Change can be approached in two ways—primarily as threat, or primarily as opportunity. I hope that this book will be of help to some in shifting the balance. The fear is real, but it need not be terminal.

These assumptions made, my prayer is that this will be a stimulating, enjoyable and ultimately useful journey.

Notes

1 Charles Handy, *The Future of Work* (Blackwell: Oxford, 1985), introduction.
2 The emerging spirituality might equally be described as post-establishment or post-orthodox. I have used the term post-Christian in an effort to remind my own faith community of the fragility of their hold on Western culture.
3 Tom Sine, *Wild Hope* (Monarch: Crowborough, 1992), introduction.

PART ONE

Root Change

An Age of Social Transformation

1

NO SMALL CHANGE

The greatest of all illusions is the illusion of familiarity.
G. K. Chesterton, *Everlasting Man*[1]

*This is a Kairos time, a time to influence and inspire our land for
a generation to come . . . May the Holy Spirit show us what may
change, what must change, and what must not change.*

Dr Sam Hutchinson[2]

Mir Christianity

This morning, you woke up on a new planet.

Imagine for one moment that you are a Russian cosmonaut, trained to endure months if not years in the weightlessness of space. The year is 1988. You are sent to live on the space station Mir, ostensibly for a period of six months.[3] But something goes wrong in the administration. You are asked to work at first a double shift and then a triple, until in the end it is over three years before you set foot again on solid ground. You are well rewarded for your hard work, and welcomed back to Earth a national hero.

But nothing has prepared you for the world to which you

return. The 'Iron Curtain' which was the defining reality of your youth has fallen. The Berlin Wall has been broken into a million pieces, carted off as souvenirs to every corner of the world. In a secret meeting in a forest dacha outside the city of Brest, Boris Yeltsin has met with the leaders of Ukraine and Belarus to frame a declaration that will tell the world, 'The Union of Soviet Socialist Republics, as a subject of international law and a geopolitical reality, is ceasing its existence.'[4] What began as a few hesitant steps of glasnost and peristroika has grown into the full-scale democratisation of Mother Russia. At least in your part of the world, communism of the one-party-rule variety is a fast-fading memory. Your universe has changed—more than you thought it could and in ways you could never have imagined. You have experienced, at first hand, the faster, wider, deeper change that is the over-arching icon of our age.

In one era and out the other

Preaching just after World War 2, at the mid-point of our century, theologian Paul Tillich spoke movingly of this flood of change and called it 'the shaking of the foundations'.[5] Fifty years later it seems that more than ever we are shaken, destabilised, by the turbulence that social change brings. Introducing its 1997 White Paper on Education, 'Excellence in Schools', the UK Government warned: 'At all levels society is undergoing massive economic, technological, social and political changes that challenge traditional values, beliefs and institutional arrangements.'[6]

Management guru Peter Drucker concurs:

Every few hundred years in Western history there occurs a sharp transformation ... Within a few short decades, society rearranges itself—its worldview; its basic values; its social and political structure; its arts; its key institutions. Fifty years later, there is a new world. And the people born then cannot even imagine the world in which their grandparents lived and into which their own parents were born. We are currently living through just such a transformation.[7]

The discovery of fire; the first ever transition from hunter-gatherers to settled community; the industrial revolution; the coming of the railways to the Western USA: previous watersheds such as these give an indication of the scope and depth of change we can expect to see.

Dee Hock, the outspoken founder of the Visa Corporation, the world's most successful virtual business, uses more dramatic imagery to make much the same observation. 'We are in the midst of a global epidemic of institutional failure,' he says, 'This next decade and maybe the one after that will be the decades that people will look back to over a thousand years and say—that was the melting pot.'[8]

Whether analysed through a theological, sociological, technological or philosophical lens, it is clear that our turn-of-the-century world is turbulent with social change.

A personal journey

My own awareness of the scale and complexity of the changes we face began in a front-line encounter with new technology in the mid 1980s. For eighteen months I served as Personnel and Training Manager for Syco Systems Ltd, in London. Syco was a high-tech retailer of musical instruments, founded in 1980 by rock star Peter Gabriel and built, initially, on the Fairlight CMI—the world's first computerised musical instrument. For several years the company led the field in the emerging technologies of computers and music. Every product carried was, in its own right, a technological breakthrough.

As Syco's Training Manager, part of my brief was to research the wider context in which the company was developing. Over a relatively short period, from 1979 to around 1986, we had seen the music industry revolutionised before our eyes. Until this point the recording of music had been based entirely on the manipulation of analogue signals—an electronic signal captured on tape as a magnetic impulse. The recording process set strict limits on what was possible in composition, reproduction and performance—much of the paraphernalia of the studio had less to do with creativity and music than with overcoming these technical limitations. In the 1970s, musicians who were computer-literate and programmers who were musically aware both began to experiment, composing and recording by an entirely new process. Sounds could be sampled by a computer and converted into digital information—the millions of binary digits on which all computing is based. This information could be manipulated almost without limit. The key was to work not with an electronic signal but with numbers. Once reconverted to the analogue domain, new sounds would then emerge for performance and recording.

Working with digital code allowed for degrees of flexibility and precision never before achieved, and the change in technology brought with it an explosion of possibilities. A simple sequence of notes could be looped to create an instant rhythm track. Drum patterns well beyond the capacity of a two-armed human drummer could be built up, layer on layer. Any sound—whether musical in origin or not— could be captured, assigned to a keyboard and converted into melody. The whole process could be delivered to disk without ever leaving the digital domain. A new language, MIDI (Musical Instrument Digital Interface), was created so that keyboards, drum machines and other instruments could talk to each other and in turn relate to PCs carrying the relevant software. A new creative landscape was opening up before the writers, performers and producers of popular music.

Fifteen years on, MIDI is a standard feature of even home-based computers, and these changes are part of music history. At the time they seemed almost miraculous. Their impact was felt immediately in all aspects of music making, transforming known styles, creating new ones and putting number-crunching at the heart of the creative process. Before long, as memory became cheaper and applications more sophisticated, it was possible to create state-of-the-art, full-scale compositions just by sitting at a work-station. The music industry would never be the same again.

The importance of this experience for me was that I saw at first hand the speed at which change could sweep through a whole domain of culture. Reading around the subject, it became clear that this new level of change was not affecting only music and musicians—it was one application or footprint of a much larger process. All around us, change on a similar scale was taking hold. And it was not just technology. Somehow, in ways that were on occasions too bizarre even to think about, these technological changes were part of, or related to, wider social changes. Attitudes were changing, and beliefs. Philosophy was involved. Religion too. A new phenomenon called the New Age Movement had grown up from nowhere and was gaining ground fast. There were political implications. Before long the Iron Curtain, that great and terrible symbol of old certainties, would fall, changing the face of the planet in an impossibly short period of time. What began for me as an object lesson in musical technology grew into an awareness of global change on a remarkable scale. My personal journey resonates with that of many others I have known or read of in recent years. I came away from the Syco experience convinced that a form of cultural meltdown had begun. Nothing that has happened since has lessened that conviction.

It is not the fact of change that demands special attention in our age—this has been implicit throughout history. It is in its order of magnitude that change is reaching new heights. Like the McDonald's empire or Michael Jordan's bank balance, change has been big for a while—but today it is bigger than ever. It is this mind-numbing volume of change that has come to mark the past two decades, and seems set to mark the next two. Put simply, change is growing faster, wider and deeper by the day.

Faster change: the shock of the new

The most helpful model for understanding the increasing speed of change remains that introduced in the late 1960s by Alvin and Heidi Toffler. The Tofflers sensed a paradox in the way technological change was affecting Western society. Technology was supposed to be delivering an upbeat future of labour-saving devices and consumer comforts, but that was not what most people were feeling. Instead, there was a strange but widespread dread in the face of life's accelerating pace. In a 1969 article the Tofflers linked this dread to 'the premature arrival of the future' and called it 'future shock'.[9] This became the title of a book in the following year, giving the Tofflers the first of many global best-sellers and introducing a new way of understanding the effects of social change.

Future shock is a form of culture shock that you experience without ever leaving home. It is defined as 'the shattering stress and disorientation that we induce in individuals by subjecting them to too much change in too short a time.'[10] It is what happens when your own culture changes so fast that you become, in effect, a foreigner within it. 'It arises from the super-imposition of a new culture on an old one. It is culture shock in one's own society.'[11] Not only will this new condition be as keenly felt as culture shock might be, but its prognosis might be very much worse. With culture shock I have the reassurance of knowing that the old, familiar world I have left behind still exists somewhere, and that one day I may get back to it. Future shock affords me no such hope. The past is gone, vaporised. The future I was hurtling towards has come to meet me head-on, and I must learn to live with it now. Even ET could phone home; the victims of future shock cannot.

The Tofflers' analysis remains relevant today, for two reasons. The first is that many people, perhaps especially in the Church, have never really caught up with this important idea. The second is that its effects are greater than ever. If future shock was already visible in 1969, when Bill Gates was chewing pencils and dreaming of becoming a train driver, how much more will it be seen and felt in 2000? Not only is the pace of change accelerating, but the rate of acceleration is itself increasing. Change is getting faster, and it is getting faster faster.

Wider change: it takes a village

Not only must we come to terms with change that is faster than ever before, we need also to see that it is wider. This operates in three distinct dimensions. Geographically, socially and culturally, the changes we presently face have a breadth to them which goes way beyond our experience to date.

Geographically wider

We are dealing, perhaps for the first time, with truly global patterns of change. There have always been changes that over a period of time spread their influence over large segments of the planet's population, but history shows this to be a slow and laborious process, taking generations to filter through. Today's changes, by contrast, are being faced simultaneously by a much higher proportion of the world's people. Marshall McLuhan's famous term 'the global village' captures this strange notion of cultural proximity overcoming geographical separation. Users of the Internet are even beginning to talk of a 'global mind', as individuals participate in new forms of discourse that know neither cultural nor national boundaries.

Socially wider

There is a social breadth to change which is breaking new ground. Every level of society is being touched, and every one of us is involved. No recent event could more perfectly express this than the incredible scenes in Great Britain in 1997 following the death of Diana, Princess of Wales. In the full glare of international publicity, the Royal Family were stopped in their tracks by a tidal wave of public emotion. Such was the strength of conviction displayed that the reigning sovereign was forced to abandon aspects of protocol that had been observed for centuries and looked set to stay for ever. No amount of wealth, nor of power, nor of prestige could preserve one of the world's most privileged dynasties from the impact of social change.

The rich and the poor; the employed and the unemployed; the owners of the means of production and the workers who own nothing; the influential and the unknown: all will be touched by the turbulence of history at this critical time. Those who walk regularly in the corridors of power, whether in politics, business or community life—or for that matter in the Church—would do well to learn by heart the mantra of change in our day: 'none of us is immune'.

Culturally wider

Thirdly, in cultural terms change is leaving a wide and growing footprint in our lives. Technological change is an obvious starting point, but it is by no means the only field of change. The need to re-imagine human culture, implied by the sheer scope of the changes taking place, will hold true for businesses, for families, for churches and social institutions. It will affect children in the classroom and their grandparents negotiating the erratic aisles of Tesco's; workers in the workplace and home-makers in the home. Town planning will change. Transport will change. The arts will change. Religion will change. Perhaps most importantly, people will change, and are changing. In assumptions and attitudes, in lifestyles and time-styles, in the relationships they build or break and the choices they avoid or make. Culturally, socially, geographically, change is getting wider by the day.

Deeper change: following the fault-line

Lastly, if change is faster than we had imagined and wider than we had assumed, it is also proving to be deeper than we at first suspected. Sociologists and cultural pundits have been used to measuring social change against a fairly short time-scale—the decade of this, the generation of that, the year of the other. But it now seems that we are seeing change that will be measured against cycles of centuries. Beliefs, traditions and practices that have held good for hundreds of years, that have been the shaping ideologies of our lives, are being questioned and revisited. Terms such as post-industrial and post-modern, which we will explore in some depth later, are an indication of this much larger time-scale.

Imagine for a moment that you live on the fifteenth floor of a tower block. You begin to become concerned because cracks have appeared in your walls, and they are widening. Your windows rattle. Your floorboards creak more than usual. In time your concern spills into action, and you begin to search for the cause. You examine the walls, to find that none of the cracks have their origin in your flat—they all begin somewhere deeper. You visit the flat on the fourteenth floor. Hearing your request, its occupant lets you know that she, too, is worried. Widening cracks; rattling windows; creaking floors—the same mysterious story as your own. But she too has established that the problem is deeper than her floor. Together, you descend to floor 13, then 12 and so on down through the building. Each floor checked confirms that the cracking has a deeper source or cause than you imagined. You end up, with fourteen of your anxious co-residents, in the basement—armed with shovel and pick-axe, hacking away at the very foundations of the building. What you initially perceived as an annoyance on a domestic scale has grown, as you have worked your way down, into something much greater. It has drawn in more and more families; its implications have magnified; you begin to sense danger. In the end it is a matter not of comfort but of life and death, affecting not your flat alone but the whole block.

This is the kind of journey that those investigating social change have found themselves taking in recent years. Every small change proves to be a symptom of some larger trans-formation, and the stakes just get higher and higher. The further back in history you go to find the source of the cracks, the greater you can assume the impact will be. It is simply not possible for a culture to abandon beliefs held for centuries and not be deeply affected. This is change comparable to the discovery that the world is not flat, change whose depth is all but unfathomable.

Faster change, wider change, deeper change: these are the parameters that mark out social transformation in our age. Together, they add up to a kind of cultural Millennopause, a 'change of life' producing a wide range of signs and symptoms and varying degrees of trauma. Beyond the transformation: new ways of living. Between here and there: changes, more changes, and changes still to come.

The X files

A social transformation of this magnitude will take several decades to run its course, and for the generations at its heart these will be decades of turbulence and uncertainty. In our own case it is those coming into adulthood in the years immediately before and immediately after the turn of the century, Generation X and the Millennials, for whom these changes will have the greatest significance. There is no clear consensus on whether the current levels of change will slow down in the foreseeable future, or whether the transitional generations will simply adapt to change and accept it as the norm. Either way, it is in the coming two decades that the river of history will cross the rapids of change, and nowhere will this have a greater impact than in the lives of these two generations. Nowhere will the cutting edge of the future, for good or ill, be sharper. All of us are affected by change, but GenX and the Millennials are at its fulcrum. We begin our exploration of a culture in transition by knocking on the door of Generation X.

Notes

1   Quoted in Roland Rolheiser, *The Shattered Lantern: Rediscovering a felt presence of God*, (Hodder and Stoughton: London, 1994).

2   Dr Sam Hutchinson, Moderator, Presbyterian Church of Ireland, opening remarks at the Coleraine Mission Conference of the General Assembly, 2020 Vision, 1997.

3   For an interactive tour of the Mir space station, visit http://www.osf.hq.nasa.gov/mir

4   Source: Michael Resnick, 'Changing the Centralised Mind', *Technology Review*, July 1994. Quoted by Prof. John M. McCann in 'Digital Dawn and Cyber Trends', http://www.duke.edu/~mccann/q-ddawn.htm

5   Paul Tillich, *The Shaking of the Foundations*, (Penguin: London, 1963).

6   Quoted by John Abbott in *'Education 2000' News*, September 1997. The 21st Century Learning Initiative http://www.21learn.org

7   Peter Drucker, *Post-Capitalist Society*, (1993), p.1.

8   Quoted by John Abbot, The 21st Century Learning Initiative, seminar presentation, 1998.

9   Alvin Toffler, *Future Shock* (Pan Books: New York, 1970). The Tofflers have recently acknowledged that both husband and wife were involved as partners in the early research and publications, even though they appeared under Alvin Toffler's name only. The partnership is acknowledged in later books. I have therefore referred to both authors throughout this book.

10   *Ibid.*

11   *Ibid.*

INTERLUDE

john one—by lynda marshall

hey, in the beginning which was before or yesterday there was the reason why. the reason why washing powder, the reason why cornflakes, the reason why trees, grass, flowers break into purple, VW Beetles, feet on babies, faces—hey, faces—there was a reason why when in a moment before now, that which was not, big black all over became . . . us.

by us i mean the one to one squillion ape-likes, wondering why they like a bad cigarette lighter were snapped into a blue second, and a moment later which was always too soon, not sometimes even able to inhale they more or less were caught and blown away.

the reason why became flesh and made his dwelling among the TV sets and buildings with no windows and we did not recognise, kept eyes on green screens, quiz shows, news, news blow over our heads, movies—good feelings, happy endings, never thinking of this end, this matchstick flame of a life we were decreasing.

hey, stood next to my shoulder this reason why, but i weren't looking over. saw him in our sid carrying a board strapped on shoulder said on it 'Jesus, Jesus'. old sid who offered me a sat-suma on a hot afternoon when i sat on a step with my heart twisted over.

'he loves you,' he said.

saw it in a girl in the classroom who we pitied because she never once rolled over with no boy in an old cortina with a bro-ken back seat. never once sucked on the stub of a cigarette until her eyes spotted, but one time, one time danced and i wasn't sure whether her feet actually touched the ground. she

had a colour on her i had never seen, it was red green purple yellow blue.
i found it in he who sat next to me unexpected on a beach and breathed into me . . .
yeah the reason why became flesh and we have seen him, the glory of the one and only, woke up life and the colours in my eyes were red green purple yellow blue purple yellow orange as the world cracked open . . .
made his dwelling within me.[1]

Notes

1   Lynda Marshall, john one (unpublished piece, 1996).

2

HOMO XAPIEN
The New Prototype

Even the much-heralded, sex-drenched 1960s look like a real dump in retrospect: cars stank, people didn't take care of their bodies, photocopiers resembled Trabants and just try finding a push-button phone to enter your answering machine's access code. Ugghh.

Douglas Coupland[1]

Our kids may be younger than us, but they are also newer. They are the latest model of human being and are equipped with a whole lot of new features.

Douglas Rushkoff[2]

The reworking of the opening chapter of John's Gospel you have just read is the work of Lynda Marshall, a twenty-four-year-old student from York. The exceptional tone of these words: rooted in contemporary culture; carrying messages both of familiarity and of strangeness; at once both prophetic and nostalgic, says two things about their author. First that she is a writer of great promise and talent. But secondly that she writes from the heart of Generation X.

It has proved notoriously difficult to define, in any

systematic way, what it is that makes GenX different, though millions of words and countless ad agency research budgets have been expended in the attempt. What pundits across the cultures of the developed world agree on is that there is something extraordinary about this age group, the children of the post-war baby-boomers. Born somewhere between 1960 and 1979, they are the last generation to come of age in the twentieth century. As with the writing of Lynda Marshall, you can spot Gen X when you see it, even if you don't know why. Bemused, pithy, streetwise, rootless, adventurous, exploratory, by turns delirious and despairing, caught between ecstasy and existential angst—GenX wander the urban jungles of the boomer generation as if they'd just landed from a far-distant planet. Like the 'family' of *Third Rock from the Sun*, they engage with the host culture without ever being fully at home—domestic life is a role to be played; planet earth is just one rock among a million; the old and familiar is new and strange and re-evaluated from a wry outsider's perspective. Fake father, fake son—is there anything you can actually call real any more?

Sales for an accelerated Coupland

Generation X was the name of a short-lived punk band in the late seventies. Over the ensuing decade, the term surfaced from time to time among media experts and ad-men struggling to win over the youth market—and encountering not so much rejection as indifference. It remained in the shadowlands of such professional specialism until 1991, when Canadian author Douglas Coupland found it, dusted it off and used it as the title for a book.

Coupland was born in 1961 and raised, for the most part in Vancouver. He travelled and studied in Hawaii, Italy and Japan and fell by chance into journalism. When his interest in the traits and trends of his own generation surfaced in an article for the periodical *Vancouver,* the concept of Generation X was born, growing up through a cartoon strip in the short-lived *Vista* magazine. Before long Coupland was asked by a New York publishing house to write a 'Guide to Generation X', modelled on the 1989 *Yuppie Handbook*. He declined the commission but accepted the hint, and moved to California to write his first novel.

Generation X; Tales for an Accelerated Culture has little by way of plot, but offers a string of snapshots of the lives of twenty-somethings Andy, Dag and Claire as they swap stories, compare disillusionment and gleefully deconstruct the strange planet, 1990, on which they find themselves. The book was an overnight success in North America, and very soon a best-seller around the world. It was closely followed by *Shampoo Planet* (1992), *Life After God* (1994), *Polaroids from the Dead* (1996) and *Girlfriend in a Coma* (1998), all of which continue Coupland's explorations of the post-boomer culture of the nineties.

While all six novels chart the journeys of the generation Coupland belongs to and has named, he has always resisted being cited as its spokesman, claiming, 'I speak for myself; not for a generation. I never have.'[3] But there is no doubt, whether by accident or design, that Coupland's work has captured the spirit and ethos of his age. He has been translated into twenty-four languages; he is quoted almost endlessly as an indispensable and insightful chronicler of the nineties; TV journalist John Fraser has described him as 'The Dalai Lama of the twenty-something generation'.[4] Generation X has become a term as widely used as 'teenager' and 'rock and roll' ever were; and many of the author's ironic definitions have effortlessly entered the linguistic gene pool. Witness, for instance, 'McJob—a low-pay, low-prestige, low-dignity, low-benefit, no-future job in the service sector. Frequently considered a satisfying career choice by people who have never held one.' Or try: 'Air Family: describes the false sense of community experienced among co-workers in an office environment'.[5] Coupland's Generation X are adrift in a world which has plenty of colour but little coherence; in which the bold dreams of its baby-boom architects have produced a hollow shell. This is a world long on options, short on substance; offering an unprecedented array of goods and experiences but little that is rooted in the permanent or meaningful. Culture past and present is a supermarket shelf of choice and opportunity; nothing is 'yours' until you choose to buy it, and then only until another purchase takes its place. Immanence is on overdrive, transcendence has taken a long holiday. Coupland quotes Al Gore as saying, 'The accumulation of material goods is at an all-time high, but so is the number of people who feel emptiness in their lives'.[6] In the newly liberated Berlin, he asks, 'What is it we can now desire, now that things, objects—stuff—have failed us?'[7] He has become one of that rare breed of writers who, by being at the right place at the right time, pen or PowerBook in hand, touch such a nerve in contemporary culture as to give a name to history. Pundits will argue endlessly on just what is so 'X' about this generation—but since Coupland, no one will say it doesn't matter.

Generation games

Broadly speaking, Generation X are those born in the 1960s and 1970s—the teenagers of the 1980s and 1990s and, by implication, the last generation to become adults before the century turns. They are approximately equivalent to the generation labelled 'Busters' by American sociologists; those born between 1965 and 1983, the children and younger siblings of 'Boomers' (1946–64) and the grandchildren of 'Builders' (1927–45).[8] Cyber journalist Douglas Rushkoff succinctly describes GenX as 'people who are too young to remember the assassination of President Kennedy and too old to have totally missed disco'.[9]

Boom or bust?

Much of the sound and fury surrounding Generation X relates to the inability of 'Boomers' to come to terms with their own progeny. GenX are not for the most part in open conflict with the institutions of their parent's generation, but they have a sophisticated and worldly-wise way of dismantling the values around which those institutions have been formed. As Kevin Ford says, 'They disregard rather than distrust authority—distrust is too active a word.'[10] Ford characterises Generation X as being shaped by three overwhelmingly negative assumptions: 'The world is not user friendly; the world is not simple; the world has no rules.'[11]

GenX co-habit the environment of their Boomer parents, but interpret it very differently. They accept the surface forms of the culture they have inherited, but divorce these from any assumed inner meaning. They will work the jobs and buy the products of the Boomer age—what they won't do is believe in it. Market analyst Karen Ritchie sums up Boomers as 'idealistic, manipulative, flashy and headstrong' and Xers as 'streetwise, pragmatic and suspicious'.[12]

For Douglas Rushkoff, this stand-off is central to the emergence of Generation X.

GenX as a term came up because a bunch of very wealthy, well-paid public relations experts kept failing to reach a certain demographic, so they went back to their bosses and said, "Oh, no, it's not us, it's not our techniques, it's this generation. They're just X; they don't care. They don't care about anything." Meanwhile these same kids have higher rates of volunteerism than during the peace corps era. It's not that they don't care, it's that they don't listen to this packaged programming anymore.[13]

The Boomer project was working; the consumer engine was purring like a Rolls—nobody expected the new generation to see things so differently. The very existence of the term Generation X points to a gulf—in lifestyle, values and understanding—between two generations which many had assumed would be continuous. Meaningful or invented, the term marks a schism in cultural history. Somewhere between the Boomer generation of Woodstock, the Isle of Wight and Watergate and the Busters of Madonna, MTV and Mcworld, a change has surfaced in Western culture significant enough to leave two generations barely able to understand one another. This is expressed clearly in the Japanese equivalent term to Generation X, *shinjinrui*—meaning literally 'a new kind of human being'.[14]

Hinge generation

The sheer scale of this schism, the depth and breadth of the Generation X divide, points to changes which run deeper by far than the so-called 'generation gap'. Something bigger is happening here than a simple evolution in fashions and values. American student worker Jimmy Long, who recently completed a PhD programme on GenX, describes his own discovery of this deeper level of change:

When I started this study project (in 1992), I was content to focus on Generation X. My goal was to study the characteristics of this generation, compare it with my baby-boomer generation, and make some suggestions for ministering to this generation. The more I studied, the more I began to feel . . . that I did not have the whole picture. Something was missing. I became more and more convinced that something more than the generational transition from boomers to Xers was affecting this present student generation.[15]

For Long, the nature of this larger change became clear through reading David Bosch's *Transforming Mission*.[16] Bosch applies scientist Thomas Khun's theories of paradigm shifts to human culture, describing the societal paradigm shifts to which history bears witness. In such shifts it is not just a generation or sub-culture but a whole culture that changes its ways of thinking and of being. It is a shift of this magnitude, Long claims, that lies beneath the GenX fault-line. The concept is captured perfectly by Graham Cray when he describes GenX as a 'hinge generation'.

Western culture is undergoing a fundamental shift. It is both a shift in the shape and organisation of society and the way people find their identity within it, and in the paradigm or world-view by which people make sense of society and make their decisions.[17]

It is this deep shift, more than fashion, trend or generational whim, that has put the X into GenX.

Straddling a cultural shift, Generation X have been raised in a context which is still engaging with the 'old', even as the 'new' is born and finds its feet. They are tied to both, just as a hinge is held to both door and door-post. If it is true, as Walter Truett Anderson says, that 'we have passed, like Alice slipping through the looking glass, into a new world',[18] then it is GenX who must make sense of the wonderland.

Behind the mirror, in a world at once both familiar and strange, both recognised and unknown, GenX must survive in a new and strange environment. Whatever the roots and routes of our social transformation—whatever the culture junction is all about—Generation X are at the heart of it.

Emigration X

It is important to take seriously this linking of GenX to a wider societal paradigm shift. For those observing the changes evident in this generation, the link is significant because:

1. It tells us that GenX aren't coming home.

The temptation with short-term generational labelling is that we simply wait for the latest generation of rebels to grow up, come to their senses and rejoin the society and culture of their parents. If GenX are, as we are claiming, a hinge generation—the last of the old and the first of the new—then such an expectation will in their case be illusory. If Gen X says nothing else to us, it says, 'Life will never be the same again.'

2. It tells us that GenX are a wake-up call to Western culture.

If the turbulence of the Generation X transition is symptomatic of a wider societal paradigm shift, then we need to move urgently from observing generational distinctives to understanding the deeper changes. GenX are significant not only for their characteristics, but also for their context —at the apex of change. Their very existence speaks to us of the transforming journey on which Western culture has embarked.

*3. It tells us that GenX are the place to start in
understanding this cultural transformation.*

If Generation X are the last of the old and the first of the
new—the hinge generation—then their attitudes and activities will be indicative, to some extent, of future directions.
In the way Generation X are thinking and behaving, and in
the choices they are making now, there will be clues as to
where our culture will move in the early years of the twenty-
first century.

*4. Generation X are the key to understanding, and perhaps
healing, the pain of the Western Church.*

For those carrying a faith-commitment, this is an added
dimension of significance to the Generation X phenomenon. One of the contexts in which Graham Cray has
applied the 'hinge generation' analogy is in the discussion of
the Post-Evangelical movement in the United Kingdom. *'Is
it possible',* he asks, *'that post-evangelicals are the Generation X or "baby-busters" of the evangelical world?'*[19] Church
leaders are wringing their hands and wondering why so
many in their twenties and thirties are asking unanswerable
questions, rejecting or deconstructing key aspects of their
faith and choosing to live out their pilgrimage in a wilderness outside of any communal church commitment. Were
they to understand better the magnitude of the cultural
transition that underpins these changes of attitude, they
might well be less discouraged and less threatened—and
better able to help.

GenX are the ice-breakers of the new, the generation at
the bow of societal change who will be the first to forge into
the emerging world. Whatever has been until now ends with
them. Whatever is to come has begun in them already.
Those of us who are concerned to anticipate the emerging

culture must start by better understanding and serving GenX. If we cannot understand GenX, we will in all likelihood fail to understand their successors. The key to winning a significant presence for the Church in the emerging culture is to win a significant presence for Generation X in the Church.

A word to the Ys

In this global transition Generation X will stand alongside those immediately beyond, their younger siblings born between 1980 and 1999. We have already called this group the Millennials: other suggested labels include Generation Y,[20] Generation Next[21] and the Mosaics[22] (in honour of their capacity to think in mosaic rather than linear forms). This is broadly the generation currently in childhood—the oldest of them slogging through school while their Generation X elders are out making sense, or nonsense, of higher education and the world of work. They will be the first teenagers of the twenty-first century, and the first generation to come of age in the Third Millennium.

Most attempts to date to ride in the wake of Coupland's 'Generation X' with an incisive profile of the Millennials are speculative and premature. It will take a Douglas (or perhaps Daphne) Coupland of 2011 to catch the zeitgeist of Generation Y. All the same, there are ways in which we can begin intuitively to reach towards the lives these post-X young people will live. Some of the key factors in this are:

1. Different already. Much of what Millennials will be is present already in what they are—the potential hidden in the actual. Even in childhood, contextual and behavioural changes can point towards the shape of teenage and adult lives to come.

2. More X than X. What has begun in GenX will go much further among Millennials—the influence of the previous culture all but wiped out by the time they reach maturity. Boomer culture will be as far removed from Millennials as WW2, Frank Sinatra and corned beef have been from GenX.

3. A new normative environment. The social influences which have been new phenomena during the lives of GenX—the Internet being the supreme example—will be taken for granted by Millennials. In an accelerated culture, the novel becomes the normal in the space of just a few years.

4. A special task. Like GenX, the context of the Millennials will greatly influence their character. Just as GenX are taking us into the change of life, it is the creativity and skill of this younger group, who will live all of their adult lives in the new millennium, that will lead us out of it.

5. Dawn of a new day. There is an important difference between living at the end of a century and at its beginning. Where GenX have lived in the apocalyptic shadow of the end of the world, Millennials will become adults in the wide open spaces of a dawning century. This may prove to be the defining factor of their age. An evening generation will give way to a morning generation.[23]

These two generations are central to our thinking about social change, just as social change is central to their lives. That which Generation X have experienced in early adulthood, the Millennials have watched as children. What they, in turn, will live through in their crucial teenage and early adult years will be the first two decades of a new century. The contours of social change by which these decades are shaped will be the contours of these new young adults' lives. In a moment we will begin to look in detail at five of those contours of change. Before doing that, though, let's allow a creative product of the 1990s to deepen our intuitive grasp of the challenges facing these junction generations.

Notes

1 Douglas Coupland, *The Past Sucks* (Short Story, 1995).
2 Douglas Rushkoff 'Playing the Future', published in the UK as 'Children of Chaos', introduction. Quoted in Internet interview, 29 May 1997, http:www.levity.com/rushkoff/bgprofile.html
3 Comment in Internet profile http://www.geocities.com/SoHo/gallery/5560/coupbiog.html
4 Comment in Internet article http://ww.nlc-bnc.ca/events/readings/couplane.htm
5 Douglas Coupland, *Generation X, Tales for an Accelerated Culture* (1991).
6 Quoted in Douglas Coupland, *Polaroids from the Dead* (1996).
7 *Ibid.*
8 See, for instance, George Barna, *The Second Coming of the Church* (Word Books: Nashville, Tn 1998).
9 Internet interview for Ziff TV, http://www.zdnet.com/zdtv/thesite/0797w1/iview/iview635jump2_070197.html
10 Kevin Ford, *Jesus for a New Generation: Reaching Out to Today's Young Adults* (Hodder and Stoughton: London, 1996), p. 122.
11 *Ibid.*
12 Karen Ritchie, 'Marketing to Generation X', quoted in Jimmy Long, *Generating Hope: A strategy for reaching the postmodern generation* (IVP: Downers Grove, Ill, 1997).
13 Comment in Internet interview for Ziff TV, *op. cit.*
14 Thanks to Lowell Sheppard for this information and translation. Such is the speed of change that a new term, *shinshinjinrui* has now appeared, describing the generation beyond Generation X as 'a *new* new type of human being'.
15 Jimmy Long, *Generating Hope*.

16 David Bosch, *Transforming Mission: Paradigm Shifts in Theology of Mission* (Orbis: Mary Knoll, 1991). Bosch's name comes up time and again as an inspiration to those seeking to understand mission to the new generations.

17 Cray et al, *The Post Evangelical Debate* (SPCK: London, 1997).

18 Walter Truett Anderson, *Reality is stranger than it used to be*, quoted in Mike Riddell, *Threshold of the Future—Reforming the Church in the Post-Christian West* (SPCK: London, 1998).

19 Cray et al, *op. cit.*

20 See for instance, *The Independent*, 23 January 1995.

21 See, for instance, the extensive Pepsi advertising campaign!

22 See, for instance, George Barna, *op. cit.*

23 Space does not allow a fuller exploration of this idea, but it is essential that we understand the difference between Generation X as a pre-millennial generation and the Millennials as post-millennial.

3

SEVEN SEAS OF WHY

It is the social transformations, like ocean currents deep below the hurricane-tormented surface of the sea, that have had the lasting, indeed the permanent, effect.

Peter F. Drucker[1]

There is no lighthouse keeper. There is no lighthouse. There is no dry land. There are only people living on rafts made from their own imaginations. And there is the sea.

John Dominic Crossan[2]

Waterworld is not a great movie by most objective standards. At its release, it was the most expensive film project in history, later surpassed by the equally watery *Titanic*. Within the industry, the on-set gossip is generally believed to be more entertaining than the script: the delays in filming due to Costner's sea-sickness; the day a freak storm sank the whole multi-million dollar set; the legendary bust-ups between the two Kevins—Costner the star and Reynolds the director. But for all the mixed reviews, there is a level at which *Waterworld* holds extraordinary power, and that is in its visual and intuitive portrayal of our contemporary situation.

Whether by default or by design, *Waterworld* offers a rich fund of imagery and nuance to better understand the junction generations. Seven images in particular set the film apart as a parable of change in our day. I offer them here not in any attempt at systematic social analysis, but more as an emotional journey—not so that we know more, but that we might perhaps feel more of the challenges these generations face.

1. A past flooded out by the future

Waterworld takes place on planet Earth, in an imagined future in which the ice-caps have melted. The world's surface has been covered by water, and those who once lived with their feet on terra firma must adapt to living at sea. This marks a subtle departure from Hollywood's habitual post-apocalyptic scenario, in which the earth is all but destroyed by nuclear holocaust, planetary collision or alien invasion. The difference in *Waterworld* is that the old civilisation has not been destroyed so much as made redundant. It remains, for the most part, intact beneath the waves. A new world has washed over the old, rendering it uninhabitable. This echoes the Tofflers' definition of future shock arising from 'the superimposition of a new culture on an old one'.[3] The survivors are those who have been lifted by the floodwaters high above what were once their roof-tops. So it is with culture shift—it is something which grows around us; begins to lift us from familiar moorings; changes us before we know we're changing. These generations are not different because of some huge, momentary crisis. They are different because a different world carries them. They are sea-borne, and the assumptions of the land-locked no longer hold the power to inspire.

2. Losing the dry ground of certainty

Waterworld's survivors must adapt to a new place in which to be human and to new ways of being human. Their points of reference, their laws, their notions of civilised behaviour, are all called into question by their sea-borne lifestyle. They float on the undulating sea, at the mercy of its winds and currents—there is no fixed point to cling to. As these generations journey through culture shift, they too are on uncertain ground. There is a rocking motion. Nausea is possible. There are storms. Structures may fall. Older generations, who have prided themselves on their capacity to survive and thrive on land, may be surprised by their own vulnerability. The sea exposes the weaknesses of those who appeared strong when they had something strong to stand on. New skills are needed for a life, for the time being, without moorings.

3. The emergence of transitional communities

Human beings are by nature culture formers. A pioneer wagon train, even if made up of total strangers, would form a defensive circle at night. Men and women are driven to band together for mutual protection and prosperity. Waterworld is no exception as new cultures and communities are formed. Some choose to bolt and buckle together their assorted floating structures to form an outer shell and, within it, to create some semblance of civic life. Others occupy huge abandoned ships, moving together across the oceans as mass pilgrims in search of a better future. Others still choose the lone call of the high seas, but live all the same by agreed codes and norms.

What these responses have in common is that they are transitional social structures. They are temporary adaptations, responding to immediate need without laying down foundations for permanence. No one knows quite what the long-term future will hold. For some, the search for the legendary 'Dryland' is enough to render any other lifestyle temporary. Equally, among the junction generations, the new cultural forms which emerge in new structures and patterns of behaviour may well be temporary and experimental. When old clothes wear out, many new outfits might be tried before the best is found. Meanwhile, we will continue to be dazed and confused by the often bizarre choices of generations in transition.

4. Be safe—be surface

Channel-hopping, net-surfing, multi-tasking, mosaic thinking, sampling, pick-and-mix: these generations are famous already for their capacity to engage with the surface level of culture but move on before getting deep.[4] This is an offence to land-dwellers, who live by laying foundations, putting down roots, digging deep. But in a flooded world, deep is dangerous. Stay too long and deep is dead. Preserving life means staying surface. These generations have learned to hop like watermites across the surface because that is the only safe way to negotiate a flood. This is not some deficiency in their attention-span, it is an appropriate adaptation to an entirely new environment. If they learn to seek internal depth, they must do it even if they remain, externally, at surface level.

> Just like ocean surfing, the habitual channel surfing of our TV-fixated youth is as lamented by parents as it is valuable to us all as an example of thriving on chaos. Just like the ocean or the man-made cityscape, the modern mediaspace, too, is a chaotic system, and subject to the same laws of dynamics.[5]

Digging is not too valuable a skill in Waterworld.

5. Plundering the past to fund the future

In one of the genuinely moving scenes of *Waterworld*,
Mariner (Costner) allows his new-found companion to join
him, via a makeshift diving bell, as he heads far below the
surface to explore the sky-scrapers and cathedrals of what
once was Dryland. No words are spoken, and the scale of the
change that has swept the planet is brought home to us in the
murky but recognisable shapes. Mariner has made it his habit
to dive deep into these flooded ruins—always surfacing with
some gadget or memento, a fragment of the old world to
bring colour to the new. This image of diving deep into the
past to seek some sign, some clue to the present and future,
is a powerful metaphor for the strange life of the junction
generations. Many in Boomer culture are surprised that
young people, with such a new and different future opening
up before them, are drawn to explore the past. In particular,
the deep history and traditions of pre-modern and aboriginal peoples are newly and unexpectedly popular. These generations sense two things above all others: that the current
culture is coming to an end, and that its replacement has not
yet fully emerged. The headteacher has announced their
retirement at the end of term, and a successor has not yet
been appointed. In the meantime, with the future unknown
and the present unreliable, the past is a storehouse of ideas to
explore. In the turmoil of today, the young rummage
through yesterday in search of keys to tomorrow.

6. Adapted to two worlds, at home in none

A sixth compelling image from *Waterworld* is that of
Mariner himself. For all that the character is defined by Costner's action-man antics, Mariner has something else that sets
him apart from the crowd. He has gills. A by-product of an

evolutionary aberration the script never quite explains, Mariner is a mutant; half-man, half-fish. He lives among the surface community, but is just as at home under water. Thus adapted to the new watery conditions of the world, Mariner is unable, when Dryland is finally located, to resettle with his human friends. As the credits roll he leaves them to their new-found paradise and sets sail, alone, for the high seas once more. No less mutant, the junction generations understand intuitively that they must live in two worlds. Generation X especially, born when the continental plates of history were already on the move, have been forced to adapt to this dual reality. Many have become bilingual, speaking the language of the past among their elders and of the future among their peers. They know just enough of both worlds to know that they are at home in neither. Rootless and restless, they wander both worlds as strangers, inexplicably driven by a longing for home.

7. And a little child shall lead them . . .

One final image from *Waterworld* which carries remarkable power at this transitional stage in history is that of the map of the future. The film's plot finds its focus in the quest for the legendary Dryland. Real or mythical, the very idea of Dryland is enough to fuel a lifetime's searching. The search, in turn, becomes centred on an old map—the only remaining clue to where Dryland might lie. But the map does not exist on paper—it is tattooed on the back of a child. Only by keeping the child with them, as they seek to understand the map, can the straggling survivors hope to reach their goal. The child, without knowing it, holds the key to the future.

This is a powerful parable for the junction generations. Though they may not know it, our children already hold the keys to reading the future. Without them, the older generations cannot hope to decode the blinding array of signals with which the new century will bombard them. The young are uniquely equipped for the environment they will meet. But they need help to read the maps they hold. The wisdom of the past without a vision of the future is irrelevant, or worse still, deadening. But a vision of the future ignorant of the lessons of the past is irresponsible. What is needed is that the two should unite, the generations overcoming the culture gap and working together to construct the new. This proves the key to success for the straggling survivors of *Waterworld*, and it stands as the best hope in our own, more real dilemmas. Many in the older generations need to face the truth that those younger than themselves hold the keys; many in the younger generations need to admit their need of help—only as the two stand together will the map of the future be intelligible. As the film's promotional slogan says, 'beyond the horizon lies the key to a new beginning'.

Notes

1 Peter F. Drucker, 'The Age Of Social Transformation', *The Atlantic Monthly*, November 1994, 53-80.
2 John Dominic Crossan, *The Dark Interval: Toward a Theology of Story* (Argus: Niles, Illinois, 1975), quoted in Richard Middleton and Brian J. Walsh, *Truth is stranger than it used to be: Biblical Faith in a Post-modern Age* (SPCK: London, 1995), p.62.
3 Alvin Toffler, *Future Shock* (Pan Books: New York, 1970).
4 The concept of surfing is probably the defining image of the junction generations, bringing together this notion of 'riding a wave' with the more physical draw of extreme sports—hence the meteoric rise of surf-related clothing brands such as Oakley, Quiksilver and Kangaroo Poo.
5 Douglas Rushkoff, *Children of Chaos: Surviving the End of the World as We Know it* (Harper Collins: London, 1997), p.39.

PART TWO

Root Causes
The Five Posts of Generation X and Beyond

The things that got you to where you are today are not the things that will get you to where you need to be tomorrow.

George Barna[1]

Picture a child's hoopla game. Two lengths of wood are joined to form an X, which lies flat on the ground. At the centre of the X, and at each of its four points, there is a wooden post—five posts in all. Players stand a short distance away and throw rope rings onto the posts, each gaining them a different points score. This is the simple visual model that we will use to describe five of the contours of the future—five key changes that make up the core of the culture junction. These five are not the only routes through the junction, but they are among the 'trunk roads' that cross it, strands of change that together will:

- ensure that the dominant culture of the West in the early years of the twenty-first century is vastly different from that of the twentieth;

- deepen and extend the changes already evident in the attitudes, preferences and lifestyles of Generation X;
- significantly shape and impact the lives of the Millennial generation as they come to maturity, and
- mark out the cultural environment within which the Christian faith community will be called to live out its witness as the century unfolds.

The five posts of the hoopla game represent five key 'posts' of the emerging age. These are the five posts of Generation X and beyond that we will explore:

- Post-industrial technology
- Post-literate communication
- Post-modern philosophy
- A post-imperial world order
- Post-Christian spirituality

Each of the five brings its own angle of analysis. Their common thread is that each speaks of change in a significant aspect of our culture. In each 'post' something is being left behind or superseded, and something new is emerging in its place. Together, the five posts form a grid or framework within which a whole range of questions about the future can be asked and answered, with the X of Generation X at its heart. The long-term shape of our culture will not be the result of any one of these transitions, but of all five held in tension. The first of the five is the 'post' of post-industrial technology.

Notes

1 George Barna, *The Second Coming of the Church: A Blueprint for Survival* (Word: Nashville, TN, 1998).

4

NEW TOOLS, NEW RULES
Post-industrial Technology

There can be no looking back. The new patterns of work are on their way whether we welcome them or not . . . they add up to a frontal assault on our view of work, the way in which it is organised and the place it occupies both in our lives and in the way that society is run.

Charles Handy[1]

In acquiring new productive forces men change their mode of production; and in changing their mode of production, in changing the way of earning their living, they change all their social relations. The hand-mill gives you society with the feudal lord; the steam-mill, society with the industrial capitalist.

Karl Marx[2]

Steam Heat

History has long acknowledged James Watt as the father of steam power. I remember being told at school that he watched his mother's kettle boil, and was inspired on the spot to invent the railway train. The truth is never that simple, but Watt was a pioneer who saw the vast potential in the everyday act of applying heat to water. His business partner, without whom he might never have left the kitchen, was Matthew Boulton, a pioneer of economics rather than of science. The inventor put up the ideas, the businessman put up the money, and in 1775 the Boulton and Watt's factory opened in Birmingham. Pushing available technology to the very limits of innovation, the factory was the first in the world to manufacture steam-powered 'prime-movers' on an industrial scale. History records Matthew Boulton's profound faith in the new venture: proved when King George 2 of England paid a visit to the site. 'Your Majesty,' Boulton said, 'I have at my disposal what the whole world demands; something which will uplift civilisation more than ever by relieving man of all undignified drudgery. I have steam power.'[3]

Fast forward 220 years. For Matthew Boulton read Bill Gates, founder of the giant Microsoft Corporation. For steam power read information processing. For the rest, the parallels are clear: the same buoyant optimism; the same zealous faith in the up-side of technology; the same potent cocktail of investment and innovation, with rich rewards for the first pioneers.

> A whole generation of us computer guys, all over the world, dragged that favourite toy with us into adulthood. We caused a kind of revolution—peaceful, mainly—and now the computer has taken up residence in our offices and in our homes.[4]

What unites this matching pair across two centuries is that they are both actors in the early years of a technological earthquake. The first industrial revolution brought mechanisation to a culture dependent on agriculture. Within decades the face of human society was substantially remodelled, until it bore little resemblance to the rural idyll of its past. Most of what we take for granted in twentieth-century culture has come to us because of this revolution—we are the children of the industrial age. The second revolution is happening now. The era of Boulton and Watts has always been referred to as *the* industrial revolution, as if we weren't expecting another, but the evidence that innovation is moving us on once again is now overwhelming:

> The law of acceleration now hurtles us into a new age. The shift from a factory-based to a computer-based economy is more traumatic even than our great-grandparents' shift from a farm-based to a factory-based economy. The Industrial Revolution extended over generations and allowed time for human and institutional adjustment. The Computer Revolution is far swifter, more concentrated, and more dramatic in its impact.[5]

The computer, which at first we mistakenly thought of as a machine because it lived in a metal box and was plugged into the wall, has become something quite different and is replacing *mechanism* with *information* as the genetic code of our economy and culture. Our world is once more in for a face-lift; change is once more at work. The early generations of Millennium 3 will be children of a second industrial revolution, and the coming two decades, at the very least, will be marked by ongoing and exponential technological change.

Definitions

The world of Generation X and beyond will be post-industrial in the sense that:

1. A primary driver of change is *technology,* in its influence on economics and the world of work and its subsequent impact on lifestyle.

2. The role of *machinery and mechanisation* as a central icon in the shaping of society has been superseded.
3. In its place, new economic, cultural and social structures are growing around the central influence of *information processing*, enabled by digital technology.
4. The influence of this new technological icon will be as widely and keenly felt as that of machine technology has been and as that of agriculture once was, shaping not just economic activities but a whole range of social and cultural structures.

Three questions confront us if we are to better understand this particular current of change:

1. **What's happening?** What is the evidence that this transition is already underway? Is this a major shift or just another flurry of inventions?
2. **What's next?** What further changes will the technologies currently in development bring? How will tomorrow's post-industrial technology be more post-industrial than the post-industrial technology of today?
3. **What's it matter?** What social forms will these changes bring? How will they impact GenX and the Millennials? What specific challenges will the spread of post-industrial technology present to our culture?

The first two of these questions will be tackled in the rest of this chapter. The third will form the basis of Chapter 6.

What's happening—the digital wormhole

It is impossible to discuss the post-industrial society without coming across the name of Peter Drucker.[6] Widely credited as the father of contemporary management studies, Drucker was raised and educated in Austria and Germany, but has lived in the United States for most of his adult life. He has been observing, analysing, informing and shaping the world of work in Western culture for over four decades, and much of this time has been dedicated to understanding the changes sweeping through industrialised cultures. Drucker's take on the whole 'technological transition' theme is that we are moving into the *'knowledge society'*.

A change in the human condition

Drucker has traced the growth and decline of the industrial revolution of Boulton and Watt by examining the types of employment dominant in society. 'By 1900,' he says, '"industrial worker" had become synonymous with "machine operator" and implied employment in a factory along with hundreds if not thousands of people.'[7] By 1950, such workers had become the largest single group in every developed country and mass-production industry was the dominant economic factor. But this peak was to be the last great hour of industrialism. In the forty years that followed, the growth of knowledge-based and service-orientated industries transformed employment and economics.

> Whereas industrial workers who make or move things had accounted for two-fifths of the American workforce in the 1950s, they accounted for less than one fifth in the early 1990s—that is, for no more than they had accounted for in 1900, when their meteoric rise began . . . By the year 2000 or 2010, in every developed free market country, industrial workers will account for no more than an eighth of the work force.[8]

In their place, our economies are now dominated by 'knowledge workers'—those whose role is not to make or move things but to process information and offer services. 'Knowledge workers . . . will give the emerging society its character, its leadership, its social profile. They may not be the ruling class of the knowledge society, but they are already its leading class.'[9]

Drucker's analysis offers compelling evidence of a major shift in the way we live and work. He is describing social and economic patterns on the grandest scale, changes that affect whole nations in their development:

> This is far more than a social change. It is a change in the human condition. What it means—what are the values, the commitments, the problems of the new society, we do not know. But we do know that much will be different.[10]

For management consultant Terence Ryan this difference can be measured in one simple assertion:

> The symbol of this new era is at hand. Today, for the first time in history, the world's wealthiest man, Bill Gates, is a knowledge worker and not a petroleum magnate, as had been the case for the past hundred years.[11]

Birth of a revolution

The transition from an industrial to a knowledge-based economy began while the old technologies were still dominant, just as industrialisation had begun when agriculture was still the majority occupation. The increasing levels of information being handled by the new knowledge workers called for new tools and a new concept—information processing. In exploring this new field, researchers began to unlock the secrets of digital code and 'computation', and before long a new technology was born. Tools invented to solve the problems of the old order served to accelerate its evolution to a new order. What began in the 1950s and 1960s as a tentative shift from *manufacture* to *information* revealed itself, with the launch of the IBM 'personal computer' in 1981, to be the revolution we now know it to be. Digital technology was not in itself the origin of this 'change in the human condition', the transition from the industrial to the information age, but it has become the driving force behind it. A society shifting from mechanism to information in the 1950s and 1960s set its sails towards the knowledge culture—and the digital technology of the eighties and nineties became the wind that filled them—a gentle breeze at first, but before long a full-force gale.

Just as mechanical technology was applied at first to making agriculture more efficient, but in time spawned whole new industries of its own, so digital technology, the child of industry, is growing up to transform the very society that gave it birth. 'The forces of digitalisation act like the gravity of a "wormhole" in *Star Trek*,' one recent report said, 'pulling recognisable industries through it and transforming them into something unrecognisable on the other side.'[12] Another prominent management theorist, Charles Handy, describes this transformation in terms of 'discontinuous change'.[13] We live, Handy argues, in the 'Age of Unreason', when each small technological breakthrough can have dramatic effects, changing us in ways from which we will never return. This is, as French magazine *Capital* proclaimed in August 1998, 'one of the fastest revolutions in human history'.[14]

Brute-force to brain-force

The recognition that the industrial age was coming to an end formed the basis of the second best-seller from *Future Shock* authors Alvin and Heidi Toffler. *The Third Wave,* published in 1980, presents 'a model of historical and social change',[15] built on the simple and compelling argument that human history has been dominated by three great waves of technology.

The first wave corresponds to the agricultural revolution which dominated human history for thousands of years. The second wave—industrial civilisation—is now playing itself out after 300 years of dominance. The Third Wave is crashing over us right now, having started with the birth of a post-industrial, high-technology, information economy in the 1950s.[16]

The Tofflers go well beyond simply telling us that this revolution is happening—they have gathered a whole range of evidence to help us see what it will mean. Their claim is that we are moving 'from a brute-force economy to a brain-force economy',[17] and that this will have enormous implications, not just for the way we work and do business, but for the way we live. Central to the Tofflers' approach is an appreciation of the extent to which our lives are shaped by the dominant technology of the day. Technology gives birth to economic activity, which in turn configures social structures and arrangements Consider, for example, the vast array of geographical, social and legal conditions that have arisen from our mastery of the internal combustion engine, of powered flight and of satellite communications. In significant areas of our lives, the tools create the rules. The hugely successful British film *The Full Monty* offered a remarkable view of this process at work. The group of men around whom the film revolves were seen to change not only their occupation, but their attitudes—to gender roles and childcare; to sexuality; to their own self-image and social role. But all these changes were rooted in a technological shift: the closing of the Sheffield steel works.

Riding the wave

When I first read *The Third Wave* ten years ago, I found myself reflecting on the extent to which machine technology had influenced the culture in which I was raised. I had to agree with the authors that mechanisation was a central icon, a kind of invisible genetic code, to industrial society. Somehow its imprint had gone beyond the immediate shaping of the industrial process—the design of assembly lines, factories and machine parts, to influence much wider social structures—schools, town-planning, housing, unions and organisations of every type, families and, yes, churches.

Terence Ryan cites the work of early industrial engineer Frederick Winslow Taylor, founder of 'scientific management', later called time and motion study, to illustrate this power of the machine as social icon. Scientific management, Ryan suggests, increased productivity 'by making each worker conform to a scientifically prescribed form of work, as mechanical as that of a machine'. The influence of this went well beyond the factory walls.

> So persuasive was the idea of scientific management, that it spread without question from the industrial sector right across all aspects of social organisations. Writing in 1910 Taylor suggested that the lessons of scientific management 'can be applied to all social activities: to the management of our homes, the management of our farms, the management of the business of our tradesmen, large and small; of our churches, our philanthropic institutions, our universities and our government departments.[18]

The limitations of such a mechanistic view of society are captured in the words of Taylor himself, who said in 1900, 'the antithesis of our scheme is asking the initiative (of our workers) . . . their workmanship, their best brains and their best work . . . our scheme does not ask any initiative in a man.'[19]

If the Tofflers, Ryan and others are to be believed, we are now experiencing the demise of these principles—the corporate, social equivalent of a heart-transplant—as information displaces machinery as the imprint at the very core of our social arrangements. The nature of this imprint—and how the information revolution will change it, is what makes the shift to a post-industrial society so important. If the adoption of machine technology has led to a machine-like understanding of work, of education and culture—even of the human condition—then what changes in understanding will the adoption of information technology bring? 'If we look back on this period in a hundred years from now,' the Tofflers argue, 'the historians will say . . . the most important thing that happened in that period was the emergence of a new civilisation. You can call it post-industrial, Third Wave or technotronic.'[20] If we are to take seriously the impact of technological change, we will need to look well beyond the realm of industry and work. Digital technology is not only changing the way we earn our keep, it is changing the way we live. In Chapter 6 we will explore the implications of this change, not least for GenX and the Millennials. But first we must take a brief look at the revolutions that are still to come, as the post-industrial 'third wave' goes beyond the boundaries of our present experience.

What's Next 1? *Cyberoptic fibrespace*

If the names of Toffler and Drucker have been associated with analysing the early decades of post-industrialism, one name that is inseparable from its future is that of Bill Gates. Head of the mammoth Microsoft Corporation and reportedly the richest man in the world, Gates has written extensively of developments that are just around the corner for digital technology. In *The Road Ahead*,[21] he gives the inside story on some of the milestones in the personal computer revolution, but stresses that the biggest leap forward remains in the future. This will be associated not primarily with *computation* but with *communication,* when the present-day Internet evolves into the 'information superhighway'.

> We stand on the brink of another revolution. This one will involve unprecedentedly inexpensive communication. All the computers will join together to communicate with us and for us . . . When communication gets inexpensive enough, and is combined with other advances in technology, the influence of interactive information will be as real and as far-reaching as the effects of electricity.[22]

Using fibre-optic cables, the 'information highway' will offer high-capacity, multi-lane links for potentially billions of users, carrying a vast array of information from one to the other. 'Fibre optics is going to render bandwidth and hertz virtually free,' techno-evangelist George Gilder has claimed, 'One thread of glass the width of a human hair can carry one thousand times the content of today's entire radio spectrum.'[23] The new network will carry not just text and voice, but broadcast-standard audio and video, full-length movies, whole libraries of reference information compressed into a few seconds of transfer-time. Cables currently being laid beneath the Pacific Ocean will have the capacity to carry 8 million voice or data conversations at any one time, compared to just 40,000 on the existing, first-generation fibre cables.[24] 'We can no more imagine what the broadband information highway will carry in twenty-five years,' Gates says, 'than a Stone Age man using a crude knife could have envisioned Ghiberti's Baptistry doors in Florence.'[25]

The advent of the information superhighway will create a whole new realm in which to live, work and make social contacts: cyberspace. A concept which first appeared in the science-fiction of William Gibson,[26] Cyberspace gets more real by the day. It is the new territory in which social inter-action will thrive. 'Cyberspace,' Michael Molone predicts, 'will be a world 21st-Century man will feel at home in.'[27] Already, business pioneers are staking their claims to Cyberspace in what Bill Gates calls 'the Internet gold-rush'.[28] 'We believe that Web sites are essentially real estate lots in an unbounded territory on a new continent,'[29] says Toby Corey, former Vice President of industry giant Novell. 'Ultimately,' says journalist Michael Moon, 'what emerges is the global Interopolis—a new, rapidly expanding republic of information.'[30]

This new revolution, that will usher in the information age for real, is still to come. The changes we've seen so far, dazzling as they are, are just the beginning, a dress rehearsal for what happens when cyber meets fibre to bring exponen-tially faster, and cheaper, communications.

> A machine that transforms communication impinges far more radically on people's lives than one that transforms computa-tion . . .You do not have to be a nerd or a mystic to see that historians will look back upon the emergence of "cyberspace" as a turning point no less decisive than the advent of the computer itself.[31]

The first adult generations of the new millennium will wit-ness, and be impacted by, the most significant development in communications technology since the creation of the alphabet. 'The information superhighway is more than a short-cut to every book in the Library of Congress,' writes researcher Nicholas Negroponte. 'It is creating a totally new, global social fabric.'[32] In Chapters 6 and 7 we will explore the impact of these changes on the ways in which we communicate, and the place in our lives of text and print. For the moment, it is crucial that we appreciate the sheer scale of this revolution, as the planet is hard-wired into a single, interactive, high-capacity communications web.

What's next 2? *The talking fridge*

Physicist Michio Kaku[33] is one of the brightest scientists on the planet. He has written extensively on superstrings, quantum field theory, hyperspace, the 10th dimension and other concepts that most mere mortals don't even pretend to understand.[34] His most recent book, a best-seller on both sides of the Atlantic, offers a guided tour of the future from the perspective of research science. Rather than blindly predict what might happen, Dr Kaku wrote *Visions: How Science Will Revolutionise the 21st Century* by asking 150 of the world's leading researchers what *is* happening. The result is a book which anticipates rather than predicts, based on research projects which are already underway and products which exist already in prototype form. *Visions* foresees three revolutions in the coming century:

- In the realm of medicine and physiology, *the biomolecular revolution* will change society forever and 'ultimately give us the power to alter and synthesise new forms of life, and create new medicines and therapies'.[35] By 2005 the Human Genome Project will have sequenced all 100,000 human genes. By 2020, a doctor will be able to take a tiny fragment of a patient's skin, analyse it and hand over a CD Rom containing a complete genetic profile. Treatment will be as likely through gene manipulation as through drugs. Diseases for which no cure currently exists will be treated genetically. Even ageing, the ancient enemy, may be rendered treatable.

- In the realm of physics, *the quantum revolution* will transform our capacity to manipulate matter. 'Nanotechnology is a field that promises perhaps the smallest of all possible machines: molecular machines,' Dr Kaku writes.[36] Invisible to the human eye, these tiny agents will perform complex tasks, opening up a whole new world of micro-management.
- *The computer revolution* will be ushered in by Moore's law,[37] which demonstrates the accelerating pace at which the production costs of computer memory are coming down.

> To appreciate the remarkable increase in computer power that is propelling us from one phase to the next, it is important to remember that from 1950 to the present, there has been an increase in computer power by a factor of about *ten billion*. At the heart of this explosive growth is Moore's law, which states that computer power doubles every eighteen months. A rapid increase in power on this scale is almost unheard of in the history of science.[38]

Once microchips cost less than a penny, below the current price of a sheet of paper, the personal computer will be replaced by millions of tiny intelligent systems, embedded in our environment: in clothes, jewellery, glasses, cars, furniture and walls. These will be voice-responsive, carrying out simple commands. In time, microchips will be as common as writing and electricity. Dr Kaku anticipates these developments within the coming two decades.

Of these three, the cyber future will be the first to be widely experienced—and the most significant to our current exploration of social change. At Media Lab—one of the world's leading research agencies, founded by Nicholas

Negroponte in 1985 and based at MIT, the Massachusetts Institute of Technology[39]—over 330 researchers work at the pioneering edge of computing. Their most cherished goal is 'ubiquitous computing'—the 'chips with everything' future that Michio Kaku is predicting, when processing power breaks out of the computer itself to be implanted in the ordinary objects of everyday life, creating a physical environment as intelligent and responsive as the motherboards of today.

> Ubiquitous computing was conceived in 1988; it may take until the year 2003 to begin to see these ideas affect our lives in an appreciable way. And it may be years after that before they reach "critical mass" and ignite the marketplace. But by 2010, one can expect to see ubiquitous computing becoming of age. By 2020, it will dominate our lives.[40]

Ubiquitous computing will put information processing at the heart of a vast array of objects and products. Processes which in current technology are essentially mechanistic, unable to respond to choice and change, will be rendered intelligent. Examples of this change can be seen in some of the products in production or foreseen even at this very early stage of the revolution. These include:

- The talking fridge—a part-pc-part-icebox that keeps everything cool but also stores recipes, offers cooking advice, and logs onto the web to transmit a shopping list.
- Intelligent ink—an electronic system with the capacity to print text into a standard book format, then refresh the content by downloading from the Internet.
- Toilets that analyse whatever lands in them and alert the user to health concerns.

- Ski-jackets with built-in communications facilities, with satellite-linked e-mail, so no skier need ever go so far off-piste that they cannot be found.
- Contact lenses that receive e-mail, and display a miniature Internet screen.
- Head-scarves that release micro-quantities of perfume when brushed against human skin.
- Robot pets—a second generation Tamogotchi, with limbs, fur and independent movement, that responds to its keeper's personality.
- A coffee machine that registers the preferences of each person in the household, and matches the drink to the voice.[41]

Ubiquitous computing will be as far beyond the current capability of PCs as domestic electricity is beyond a first-generation steam traction engine. It will take the impact of digital technology, the shift from machines to information, and spread it into every corner of our lives. Whatever else it achieves, the 'chips with everything' revolution will increase and deepen the impact of the 'Third Wave' technological shift.[42]

These two 'revolutions yet to come', the information highway and ubiquitous computing, will consolidate the place of information processing at the very heart of the twenty-first century. Digital technology, as it evolves, will be one of the most powerful shaping forces in the lives of the transitional generations. As much as the twentieth century has reflected the characteristics of industrial mechanism, so will the twenty-first reflect information processing—from the macro-scale of multi-national corporations to the micro-scale of a lone teenager logging onto the web. It's time to ask, 'What's it matter?' What are the implications of the information revolution for the Homo Xapien experience?

Notes

1 Charles Handy, *The Future of Work* (Blackwell: Oxford, 1985), introduction.

2 Karl Marx, *The Poverty of Philosophy*, quoted in James Robertson, *The Sane Alternative* (Robertson: Oxford, 1983).

3 Sigvard Strandh, *A History of the Machine* (Arrow Books: London, 1984), p.150.

4 References taken from Bill Gates, *The Road Ahead*, electronic version—http://www.roadahead.com

5 Arthur Slessinger Jr, 'Has Democracy a Future?' in *Foreign Affairs*, September/October 1997, quoted in Terence Ryan 'The Changing Economy, Information Communication Technology and New Forms of Business Management: What They Could Mean for Education Systems.' Paper for the 21st Century Learning Initiative, April 1998. www.21learn.org

6 See http://www.pfdf.org

7 Peter F. Drucker, *op. cit*, pp. 53-80.

8 Ibid.

9 Ibid.

10 Ibid.

11 Terence Ryan, *op. cit*.

12 P. William Bane, Stephen P. Bradley and David J. Collis, 'Winners and Losers: Industry Structure in the Converging World of Telecommunications, Computing and Entertainment', Multimedia Colloquium 1995, Harvard Business School. Quoted by Prof. John M. McCann in *Digital Dawn and Cyber Trends*.

13 Charles Handy, *The Age of Unreason* (Arrow Business Books, 1991), quoted in Danny Brierley, *Young People and Small Groups* (Scripture Union: Bletchley, 1998).

14 *Capital*, no. 83, August 1998, p. 42. 'Nous sommes en train de

vivre une des révolutions les plus rapides de l'histoire humaine.'

15 Interview, *New Scientist*, 19 March 1994, pp. 22-25, quoted at http://www.physics.wisc.edu/~shalizi/NewScientistArticles/alvin-toffler

16 Ibid.

17 Ibid.

18 Robert Kanigel, *The One Best Way* (Viking Penguin: New York, 1997), quoted by Terence Ryan, *op. cit.*

19 Ibid.

20 Interview, *New Scientist*, 19 March 1994, pp. 22–25, quoted at http://www.physics.wisc.edu/~shalizi/NewScientistArticles/alvin-toffler

21 References taken from Bill Gates, *The Road Ahead*, electronic version. http://www.roadahead.com

22 Ibid.

23 George Gilder, quoted in Stephen L. Talbott, *The Future Does Not Compute: Transcending the Machines in Our Midst* (O'Reilly). Available at http://www.ora.com/catalog/future/excerpt/cho6.html

24 'The World in 1999', the *Economist*, November 1998.

25 Bill Gates, *op. cit.*

26 Gibson introduced the term in his 1984 novel Neuromancer, after watching young people in a games arcade hunch over their games as if caught up in an imaginary space beyond the screen. Ironically, Neuromancer was written on a manual typewriter. ref: National Geographic, 'The Information Revolution', October 1995.

27 Michael S. Malone, 'Chips Triumphant', Forbes ASAP, 26 February, 1996, p. 74, quoted by Prof. John M. McCann in Digital Dawn and Cyber Trends http://www.duke.edu/~mccann/q-ddawn.htm

28 Bill Gates, *op. cit.*

29 Jim Mallory, 'Former Novell Execs Launch Web Venture, *Newsbyte News Network*, 18 December, 1995, quoted by Prof. John M. McCann, *op. cit.*

30 Michael Moon, 'Dirt-Cheap Bandwidth and the Coming Revolution', *Electronic Buyer News*, 31 January, 1994, p. 44, quoted by Prof. John M. McCann, *op. cit.*

31 'That Astonishing Microchip', the *Economist*, 23 March, 1996, quoted by Prof. John M. McCann, *op. cit.*

32 Nicholas Negroponte, *Being Digital* (Alfred Knopf, 1995), p. 181, quoted by Prof. John M. McCann, *op. cit.*

33 For an exploration of Michio Kaku's work, see http://www.wbaifree.org/explorations/index.html

34 Dr Kaku can be contacted at mkaku@aol.com Information and bibliography available at http:www.dorsai.org/~mkaku/

35 Michio Kaku, *Visions: How Science Will Revolutionise the 21st Century and Beyond* (Oxford University Press, 1999).

36 Ibid.

37 'This was first stated in 1965 by Gordon Moore, co-founder of the Intel Corp. It is not a scientific law, in the sense of Newton's Laws, but a rule-of-thumb which has uncannily predicted the evolution of computer power for several decades.' Michio Kaku, *op. cit.*

38 Ibid.

39 http://web.mit.edu

40 Michio Kaku, *op. cit.*

41 Examples drawn from: *Focus Magazine*, February 1998, 'The Men Who Really Know Your Future', and *Capital Magazine*, no. 83, August 1998, 'Comment Nous Vivrons dans Vingt Ans'.

42 I have deliberately avoided, throughout this chapter, making judgements on whether new technology is a 'good' or a 'bad' thing for society. Melvin Kranzberg, the American historian of technology, hit the nail on the head in forming what he calls Kranzberg's First Law: 'Technology is neither positive, negative nor neutral'. A major debate *is* needed lest the 'techno-evangelists' lead us into a fools' paradise or the technophobes keep us out of a real one. Our purpose here is not to hold that debate, but to identify as objectively as possible the changes that are happening and their likely impact. The world that will be will be, whether we approve of it or not.

5

HIGH-CYBER DIET
Living with Post-industrial Technology

It is not only our material environment that is transformed by our machinery. We take our technology into the deepest recesses of our souls. Our view of reality, our structures of meaning, our sense of identity—all are touched and transformed by the technologies which we have allowed to mediate between ourselves and our world.

David Lochhead[1]

You can no longer remain unconscious where you slept before; one way or another, you are creating your future. Wake up before you find that the devils within you have done the creating.

Stephen L. Talbott[2]

Technological change does more than thrust upon us a new set of tools. It invites us, tools in hand, to participate in the reshaping of society. The growth of 'new technology' is relevant to more than just commercial interests. In a complex chain of relationships that takes in economic activity, demographics, social structures, educational provision and domestic arrangements, a shift in technology sends out coded signals that trigger a cascade of other changes.

Signals that reflect, somehow, the nature of the technology at work. If the processing of information is different in essence from the manufacture and sale of goods, then the culture which grows up around it, the information society, will be a very different culture. It will bring changes in behaviour and values right across the post-industrial world: changes that are already surfacing in the lives and attitudes of Generation X and the Millennials. It will be to these changes that the church of century 21 will be called to respond. This chapter will explore three of the key changes that this journey will bring.

1. The triumph of hyperchoice

Post-industrialism will dismantle many aspects of the industrial age, but the consumer economy is not one of them. What the industrial society has aspired to in terms of consumer choice, digital technology is at last able to deliver. The customer is king, and has almost unlimited choice of where to spend, and what on—with the miracles of information processing to cope with the complexities of servicing the choices made. This age of hyperchoice consumerism is upon us.

What is true in the market-place of goods and services is spilling over into the market-place of ideas, with philosophical and religious choices increasingly subject to the same consumer criteria. Today's credal consumer browses the shelves of the faith hypermarket, unwilling to make a purchase until her customer needs—personal, specific and complex—have been fully met. Every attempt to force a sale is repelled with the mantra of the age, 'I still haven't found what I'm looking for.' Shop around; try before you buy; check out the brochure; keep your consumer options open: the philosophical shoppers of post-industrialism are as tough to please as a customer ever was. What they come to expect in the marketplace, they will increasingly also expect in their relationships with social institutions, including the Church.[3] Some of the implications of hyperchoice consumerism in the realm of faith are:

Acceptance of competition as normative

In many areas of life, competition was once a dirty word. In hyperchoice consumerism, it is seen as the necessary companion of quality and value. For better or worse, the economies of the developed world are shifting more and more into a hyper-competitive free market. The spill-over of this development into the realm of faith and ideas does not mean, by definition, that churches must compete with one another—all institutions have a choice as to where they operate on the competition / co-operation continuum. What it does mean is that their customers—their members and potential members—are more likely to have checked out the competition, and will reserve the right to choose from a competitive short-list. Describing the fast-growing 'megachurch' phenomenon in America, Charles Trueheart writes:

> In spontaneous imitation of that other late-century cathedral, the mall, the megachurch offers a panoply of choices under one roof... from worship styles to boutique ministries, plus plenty of parking, clean bathrooms and the likelihood that you'll find something you want and come back again.[4]

An increasing hunger for experience

The experience of buying has become more important than the product bought, leading to the assertion that '*the experiential consumer*' has arrived. What is true in commerce and industry is also increasingly true in leisure, in relationships and in religion—it is experience rather than content that provides the criteria by which a social transaction is evaluated. The generations of the post-industrial twenty-first century will increasingly evaluate every product, including public faith, in terms of their experience of it.

Loyalty is earned, not given

One of the features of hyperchoice consumerism is the loyalty programme. Air miles, clubcard points, fidelity schemes—almost every industry sector that thrives on repeat business is working to create rather than assume loyalty. The principle is that 'a single purchasing decision does not commitment make'. Consumers not only have the right to put their initial business wherever they want to: they reserve the right to switch horses at whatever stage in the race it seems beneficial to do so. What will this mean in the realm of faith? That we can expect to see increased 'horse-switching' in terms of congregational, denominational and even credal commitments. And that we can expect faith adherents to self-audit their experience more frequently. I made the decision then, but is it still working for me now? Loyalty is not absent in GenX and the Millennials, but it will be a hard-won prize.

Made-to-measure expectations

At its height the industrial age was marked by the mass production of standardised goods, immortalised in Henry Ford's words, 'You can have it in any colour you want, as long as it's black.' More recent developments have worked towards greater diversity and increased design options. In many industries, digital technology is now delivering a level of consumer choice which comes close to made-to-measure solutions. This raises customer expectations and creates suspicion of standard designs, off-the-shelf solutions and ready-made packages. What works for customer A may not work so well for customer B, and those who provide services are increasingly expected to adapt them to the individual.

It ain't sold until I buy it!

The customers of hyperchoice consumerism are self-aware, well-informed and in control. They want product information, they will seek sales advice—but they will not be coerced into a purchase. The self-service megastores of Virgin and Ikea are as much a symbol of this new age as door-to-door insurance salesmen were of the old. Hyperchoice consumers want to see what's on offer; they want to ask difficult questions about it; they want time and space to reflect without pressure. The first sign of a pressurised sale will having them saying 'no' just for the sake of it. 'Techniques of coercion and trying to coerce a culture aren't going to work any more,' Douglas Rushkoff has said 'What you have to do is just make a good product, tell us what it does and charge a good price.'[5]

2. Asynchronous lifestyles and timestyles

The standard definition of a machine is that formulated by German engineer Franz Reuleaux (1829–1905): 'A machine is a combination of solid bodies, so arranged as to compel the mechanical forces of nature to perform work as a result of certain determinative movements.'[6] 'Solid' . . . 'arranged' . . . 'determinative' . . . a machine can only achieve its allotted task with the right components in the right place at the right time. For an assembly line to operate, it is necessary that a set number of workers present themselves for duty at the set time and work at the line's designated pace until the set time to finish. Built as it is on machine technology, the growth of industrialism throughout Western culture brought with it an increased emphasis on determined, synchronised movement. Engineers such as Frederick Wilson Taylor brought new profits to employers through their systems of 'applying machine-type processes to human labour'[7], kicking off a chain reaction that resulted in 'Newton's concept of the perfect machine . . . fully realised and expanded into the human sphere'.[8] Industrial society became dependent on spatial and temporal synchronism— a large number of people being in the same place at the same time. Commuting, the rush hour, terraced housing, the school timetable, bank holidays, shopping hours—all these are spin-off products of industrialism's need for fixed times and places. When an assembly-line is the culture's idea of excellence, uniformity, standardisation and synchronism will rule.

Digital technology is undoing this with great speed. As Paul Saffo, Director of the Foundation of the Future has said, It is 'the solvent leaching the glue out of old, much-cherished social, political and business structures'.[9] Social interaction no longer requires geographical proximity, nor synchronous timing. An e-mail network might draw together participants from every continent; a web-page will sit, available to all, day and night. The new standard for customer service is 24/7—24 hours a day, 7 days a week. Supermarkets are following suit with 24–hour opening. The global credit clearance systems operate all hours, making 'banking hours' a quaint memory. Telephone service centres in Dublin or Barcelona will handle customer calls rerouted from every part of Europe. A business on one side of the Atlantic will down-load its day's trading figures to a data-processor on the other, to be computed 'overnight' and presented as summarised accounts before the opening of business the following 'day'. More and more workers are offered flexi-time contracts; more and more professionals are 'tele-commuting'. It is less and less likely that you will live next door to someone who lives according to the same timestyle as you do.

One of the slowest institutions to become aware of this change, it seems, is the Church, which for the most part still assumes that the faithful will gather in a fixed place at a fixed time. A minority of churches are breaking the pattern, but it remains true that for the vast majority Sunday is the day on which God's business is done. To outside observers, a Sunday congregation is the primary visible manifestation of church. Church is a physical place that people 'go to'. Like an industrial plant, the Church seems able to function only if its 'components' are in the right place at the right time. For many churches, the pattern even pre-dates industrialism, stemming from an era in which most of the congregation lived, worked, married, bore children and died without ever leaving the parish. Leith Anderson points out in *Dying for Change*[10] that most American churches meet at a day and hour suited to the needs of dairy farmers—they just have time to get the milking done before the family outing 'to church'. Anderson muses, as a contemporary church leader, that neither he nor the vast majority of his congregation have ever milked a cow in their lives.

If the Church continues to insist on synchronism in an asynchronous culture, it will lose contact with the growing numbers of people whose lifestyle and timestyle patterns no longer fit the old norms. With timestyles personalising and diversifying, it will be increasingly difficult for a local church ever to gather all its members in one place. A church which genuinely adapts to post-industrial culture will find that it must accept:

The end of roll-call worship

Being visible in a Sunday congregation will no longer be the acid test of commitment. Being 'all together in one place' will be the exception rather than the norm, and may never happen. So what will being a member mean?

The end of one-size-fits-all ministry

Congregations as diverse as a Tuesday morning shoppers drop-in, a Friday night pub discussion group and a cyber-linked Diaspora will all seek the support and blessing of the same local church structures. Will those structures have the necessary flexibility to respond?

Discipleship through mousegroups

If cyberspace grows to become a genuine meeting place for the community,[11] pastors will find themselves building relationships with people they have never met, and perhaps never will. Do we have ministry models that will cope with this?

The end of the 'local' church?

In a geographically diverse culture, 'local' is increasingly defined in terms of interest-group rather than neighbourhoods. Can the Church accept this as a valid basis on which to build congregations? 'People don't work in their neighbourhoods,' says Bill Bruford 'People don't shop in their neighbourhoods. People don't go to the movies in their neighbourhoods. So why should anyone expect them to go to church in their neighbourhoods?'[12]

The end of synchronism does not simply mean that everyone will opt out of church in the 'real world' and head off into virtual reality. It is not about the demise of the physical church. But it does mean that the physical church will have to become more flexible, diverse, adaptable and responsive than it has been for many generations. 'The mainline denominations are bleeding,' writes Charles Trueheart. 'Their churches have more pew than flock, and unless they change, they have more history than future.'[13] To adapt to changing times will not mean becoming less biblical, but more so. The Jerusalem church of Acts 2, in which 'Every day they continued to meet together in the temple courts. They broke bread together in their homes and ate together' (Acts 2:46, NIV) represents almost certainly one of the most adaptable, open-to-change communities ever.

3. Migration from suburbia to cyberia

'Cyberia' is the name given by author Douglas Rushkoff to the world inhabited by users of the Internet.[14] It is cyber-space once it has been colonised.

> In America we've destroyed virtually every civic space, and in the UK you don't have much more. America is suburb strip mall hell. There's nowhere to go and nothing to do. I see interactive media as a remedial help for a society that really doesn't have any more open conversations. I think it's working for young people as a community space.[15]

More and more people are being drawn to this 'new place to be', not just to do business but to interact socially, to build relationships, to make human contact. As cyberia becomes more populated, it will present the Church with a new and uncharted missionary challenge. How can the Church become incarnate in the cultures of cyberia? It will only do so by recognising the importance and urgency of the need.

Last time around, rural church leaders and members took generations, almost centuries, to accept that industrialisation and urbanisation were transforming human culture and that a response was needed. Thousands upon thousands of workers and their families were left to migrate into the cities without the pastoral support of the Church. Where the churches did respond, they often did so by transferring to the urban context the models, concepts and calendar of ministry that had worked so well in the countryside for generations. No wonder the years of urbanisation have been years of decimation for the Christian faith. Even today, many church congregations cling to rural models of faith that are irrelevant, and redundant, in the communities in which they live and work. Procrastination gripped the Church again when 'youth culture' first emerged in the post-war years. Only through the visionary determination of pioneers such as Billy Graham were the new 'youth missionary' organisations born. As culture moves on once more, and thousands migrate to cyberia,[16] we need to face the challenge sooner, faster and more effectively than our forebears. We will only do this by:

Taking the territory seriously

William Carey had to spend years persuading his fellow-Baptists that Africa and India mattered. We may face a similar battle for cyberia, but we must recognise now that it is a real place; that people live there; that it is a milieu in which matters of faith can appropriately be expressed.

Learning the language and culture

Contemporary missionaries know that they must be skilled in cultural anthropology: that they must listen, learn and understand before ever they have the right to speak. If Cyberia grows to become a significant continent of century 21, we need a generation of missionaries to begin their learning process now.

Letting go of 'oldworld' assumptions

If cyberia offers a new language to learn, it also challenges us to unlearn the old. Those working to carry the life of the Church into cyberia will have to abandon many habits, assumptions and distinctions. In cyberia, for instance, there is no 'abroad'—home and overseas are one seamless unity and mono-cultural groupings virtually impossible. Cyberia is an egalitarian society, at least in terms of access and the right to speak. The opinions of a learned professor take just as many bytes to transmit as those of a creative novice—and in many cases you won't know which you are in touch with. Neither are age distinctions visible in cyberia—it has no 'youth' culture. Some distinctives of cyberia are trivial, others fundamental—the new country will demand of you that you abandon long-cherished assumptions from the old.

Aiming for an indigenous church

I have no idea what church-planting in cyberia will mean, but I do believe that we will need to do so, and that there will be a section of the next century's population who will not join any other church. Internet mission is about more than buying web-space to advertise existing churches. Don't go to cyberia to plant churches for suburbia.

Mobilising GenX and the Millennials

Cyberia is a young space. Not all those born since 1960 would claim to be more at home there than anywhere else—but some are, and most have a more immediate, intuitive grasp of the culture than their elders. Many are bilingual, living daily in both suburbia and cyberia, fluent in the language of the Church and the language of the Web. Many churches are losing these young people because they don't value or validate their cyberian experience. In doing so, they lose not only the individual but a potential link into this new, emerging world. The Church's own GenX and Millennials need permission, and with it encouragement and resources, to be pioneer missionaries to cyberia.

The rise of cyberia, the end of synchronism and the triumph of hyperchoice will be three 'big apples' in the fruit basket of the post-industrial society. All three will deeply influence the emerging generations, presenting new and unique challenges to the Church. There will be other significant changes, and somewhere in all of them the imprint of digital technology will be seen. In summary, the years ahead will be post-industrial in the sense that they:

- Will see the ongoing progress of the revolution that has already begun, the transition from the industrial society dominated by machine technology to the knowledge society, dominated by information processing.
- Will be further rocked by two yet-to-be revolutions: the advent of cyberia, when billions of computers go live on a super-fast, broadband, globally interactive network, and the growth of ubiquitous computing, when chips are embedded in every nook and cranny of our homes and surroundings, extending the impact of digital technology and rendering the human environment intelligent.
- Will see a remodelling of social and cultural institutions and norms in ways which reflect this shift from an industrial to a post-industrial paradigm.
- Will witness in the maturing of Generation X and the coming-of-age of the Millennials, the emergence of cultural and behavioural patterns shaped by the new technological paradigm.

The information revolution is not only dismantling the social structures of the industrial age and undermining mechanisation, it is also on the verge of dethroning another age-old technology. It is a technology that has dominated Western society not for three centuries but for five—some would say since 1438—and runs so deeply through our culture that it is hard to imagine life without it. But imagine it we must. The writing is on the video wall—the future is a whole new chapter for the book.

It is to this second 'post' of the emerging world that we now turn.

Notes

1 David Lochhead, 'Technology and Interpretation: A Footnote to McLuhan', Internet article, http:www.interchg.ubc.ca/dml/martin.html First published in *Journal of Theology* (Dayton: United Theological Seminary, 1994).

2 Stephen L. Talbott, *The Future Does Not Compute: Transcending the Machines in Our Midst* (O'Reilly). Available at http://www.ora.com/catalog/future/excerpt/cho6.html

3 This section does not represent a detailed critique of consumerism, which has both positive and negative elements. For better or worse, hyperchoice will shape the expectations of twenty-first-century consumers, and therefore must be taken seriously as an influence on our culture. For a more in-depth analysis of consumerism, see Mike Starkey, *Born to Shop* (Monarch: Crowborough, 1989); Oliver James, *Britain on the Couch—Why we're unhappier than we were in the 1950s, despite being richer* (Arrow Books: London, 1998), and (http://cgi.pathfinder.com/time/magazine/1997/int/970922/essay.puting_britai.html) and Tom Sine, *Mustard Seed vs McWorld* (Monarch: Crowborough, 1999).

4 Charles Trueheart, 'Welcome to the Next Church', *Atlantic Monthly*, August 1996.

5 Douglas Rushkoff, 'On Cyberculture' interview for Ziff Davis TV Inc. http://www.zdnet.com/zdtv/thesite/0797w1/iview/iview635jump3_070197.html

6 Quoted in Sigvard Strandh, *A History of the Machine* (Arrow Books: London, 1984), p.6.

7 John Abbot and Terence Ryan, 'Can This Really Ever Happen', *The Journal of the 21st Century Learning Initiative*, March 1998. Available at http://www.21learn.org Abbot and Ryan's article presents a consistent and compelling analysis of the impact of mechanisation on the wider culture, and on education in particular. Looking to a post-mechanistic future, they say 'The question of battery hens or free-range chickens is critical to a nation's future excellence.'

8 *Ibid.*

9 Paul Saffo, Interview by PBS Frontline, 12 June 1995, quoted by Prof. John M. McCann in Digital Dawn and Cyber Trends, http://www.duke.edu/~mccann/q_ddawn.htm

10 Leith Anderson, *Dying for Change* (Bethany House Publishers, 1989).

11 Some challenge the notion that there can be real community on the Internet. See, for instance, chapter 6 of Stephen L. Talbott, *op. cit.*, for a sobering reminder of the limitations of on-line relationships ('Community is ... something to be salvaged from information technology, not furthered by it.') My own experience of eighteen months as a member of a 'cyberpub' discussion group has been very positive. Where cyber-relationships are complemented by other forms of contact, I believe that the 'virtual' element can reach unexpected depths. But cybertouch will never be a total substitute for 'skin'.

12 Bob Bruford, Texas businessman and author, founder of Leadership Network, quoted in Charles Trueheart, *op. cit.*

13 Charles Trueheart, *op. cit.*

14 Douglas Rushkoff, *Cyberia: Life in the Trenches of Hyperspace*, 1990.

15 Douglas Rushkoff, 'Lost In Translation', interview with Chris Mitchell, http://www.hedweb.com/spike/0297rush.htm

16 To say that people 'live in' cyberia is to assert that they increasingly see it as their primary arena of social contact.

The expectation that those people will be cranky and isolated and switched off from seeking physical community is proving unfounded. Rushkoff says of the 'rave' scene—the first genuine spin-off of cyber culture—'the fact remains that the first real cultural outgrowth of the computer revolution did not turn out to be the solitary, non-physical experience that many had feared. If anything, it is a reclamation and assertion of the body in the face of our seemingly mechanised computer lifestyles. There is most definitely a thriving cyberculture gaining influence around the world. You just have to get off the computer and out of the house to experience it.' (Interview for Ziff Davis TV Inc., *op. cit.*) The challenge to the Church is to understand that these people live and breathe the culture of cyberia.

6

GUTENBERGER AND CHIPS
Post-literate Communications

Of all the issues associated with the information explosion—such as privacy, copyright, libel and computer theft— the battle of the book may have the greatest impact.

Joel L. Swerdlow[1]

Our books better communicate something more than a Web page does, too. We have to understand what it is a book can do . . . or quit cutting down trees for no reason.

Douglas Rushkoff[2]

Taps and buckets

When I was a little over two years old, my parents bought a cottage in County Wexford, Eire: one of around twelve dwellings stretched along a mile of pot-holed lane. Electricity was connected, mains water was not. The farmer at the top of the lane was fortunate enough to have a well in his yard: everyone else had two choices for obtaining fresh water. The first was to collect it in barrels whenever it rained, the second was to walk or cycle half a mile to the nearest municipal pump. On our property, my father arranged for a deep well to be drilled, an electric pump to be installed and piping and drainage to be laid. Ours was the first home on the Ford of Ling to have hot and cold running water.

What strikes me in the distant memory of this time was the effect that the limited supply of water had on those forced to live with it. The barrels and buckets of collection and delivery were a valued part of daily life. Different sources of water were allocated to different tasks—pumped water for drinking, rainwater for washing, ditch water for the livestock and flowers. Children were taught early to treat water with respect, and not to waste. Such was the value of fresh water that our nearest neighbour, a merchant seaman with a good line in Polish vodka, would regularly swap my father two bottles for a bucketful.

All this changed, overnight, when mains water was installed. The old barrels were left to rot, or painted up as ornaments; gossip at the village pump had to find some other focus; domestic routines were transformed. Who would heat a tin bath in the kitchen when there's a fitted bathroom upstairs? What girl will wash her hair once weekly in rainwater when she can wash it every day over the sink? The simple technological shift of making that which came in bucketfuls available on tap changed everything for this rural population. And if information is water, and books are buckets, much the same is happening to us now. We have collected knowledge by the barrel-load—very soon it will be there for us on tap.

The Gutenberg galaxy

We have already seen that the marriage of computing power with fibre-optic technology and ultra-cheap communications links will create a whole new media realm—the new land of cyberia. A wide range of commentators are now comparing this moment to the birth of the print age, and suggesting that we are becoming 'post-literate'.

The era of literacy was born in 1438, when 'Johannes Gutenberg wanted a cheaper way to produce hand-written Bibles. His movable type fostered a spread in literacy, an advance of scientific knowledge, and the emergence of the industrial revolution.'[3] The breakthrough into print technology had an almost immeasurable impact on Western culture. According to communications theorist Marshall McCluhan, it carried us into 'the Gutenberg Galaxy'.[4] For Mcluhan, 'print as a technology is the catalyst that allowed the emerging mechanistic, linear, individualistic tendencies of the modern period to become the integrated, dominant pattern of our time'.[5]

The electronic era is something else entirely—a culture dominated not by the printed word but by multi-media, interactive, free-flowing information. The revolution which began with broadcast radio, gathered pace with television and found a running-mate in satellite and cable capabilities, will hit break-neck speed in cyberoptic fibrespace. The final effect this will have on the ways we think, communicate and learn is as yet unknown—the information revolution is still young. But it is clear that there *will* be an effect. If we are concerned to relate to the world of the new century; if the lives of Generation X and the Millennials mean anything to us, then we must give time to exploring the implications of this shift beyond the literate. We are about to leave the Gutenberg galaxy, travelling at warp speed. Can we even begin to anticipate what new corner of the universe we will arrive in?

Definitions

The world of Generation X and beyond will be post-literate in the sense that:

1. A primary driver of change will be the changing *communications media.*
2. The role of *printed text* as the primary medium of communication, of learning and of information storage and transfer, is superseded.
3. In its place, new cultural, educational and popular forms emerge around the availability of *interactive media,* made possible by digital technology.
4. The impact of this technological shift will be widely and keenly felt—in the ways people learn, the ways they communicate and in the shape and nature of the ideas that influence them.
5. The emergence of new communication paradigms will be seen first in the transitional generations: caught in the tension of dual citizenship; speaking the old language, but increasingly attracted to the new.

Our purpose in this section will be to explore this 'change of galaxies', and to ask:

- What are the key differences between print-based communication and interactive media?
- What effect will these differences have on the transitional generations?
- What challenges will this present to the Christian faith community?

Once again, we will deal with the first two of these questions in the current chapter, leaving the important themes of the third to Chapter 8.

The virtual McCoy

It is fairly straightforward to describe just what it was that Gutenberg hit on—the dissemination of ideas and information through printed text. The methods were slow at first, but soon gained the speed and capacity of a bulk technology, creating human culture's first experience of mass communication. Print technology's abiding symbol is the book—a bound and defined repository of words, associated with authority, learning, scholarship and sophistication. Post-literacy, fast replacing print as the dominant communications ethos, is not the result of any one technological change, but of several. These include:

- The shift from word to image, as transmitted by photography, TV, video and the computer screen and empowered by digital technology's image-manipulation capacity and bit-stream delivery.
- The transition from text to hypertext brought by the computer's capacity to both write and read in non-linear forms.
- The power of digital technology to combine word, image and sound as multi-media information.
- The inter-connectedness and interactivity of cyberia.
- The relative ease with which a PC, CD-Rom drive and modem puts all this into the hands of the individual.

The dominance of image has been with us for some time—initially in cinema, more recently in television and supremely in the advertising industry both have played host to—but it is the power of digital encoding, unlocking the problems of bandwidth, speed and capacity, that signals most strongly the end of the print age. If there is any one development that history will credit as decisive in this leap, it is likely to be the marriage of cyber and fibre referred to in Chapter 6—the birth of 'cyberoptic fibrespace'. But the impact of these changes on human culture and behaviour, already visible in GenX and the Millennials, rests with the combined influence of these different elements. Post-literacy is not a single drink but a cocktail; the taste of instant communication blending with the potency of the moving image, laced with the spice of interaction.

Some of the characteristics of the post-literate era that will set it apart from the age of print are:

1. Capacity and scope

In terms of storage

When Bill Gates wanted to demonstrate the storage capacity of the CD Rom, he had himself photographed sitting on a fifty-five-foot high pile of paper. 330,000 sheets of single-spaced text could still not match the CD's hunger for information. With more encyclopaedias now being sold in digital format than as books, the huge reference potential of the medium is clear. Add to that the development of DVD technology and the increasing possibility of down-loading direct from the Internet, and the measure of information instantly available to a PC-user starts to run into millions, rather than thousands, of pages.

In terms of experience

Computers offer more than just reference information. Cyberpunk author William Gibson says that electronic communication provides 'a sensory expansion for the species by allowing people to experience an extraordinary array of things while staying geographically in the same spot'.[6] Those who have tended to use the term 'virtual reality' in a dismissive sense—to describe a reality that is less real than real reality—may need to think again as increasing numbers find it very real indeed. Cyberia is a *different* reality but for those who experience it, it is no less real.

In terms of access

The electronic arena puts something approaching broadcast technology in the hands of the individual citizen. Bill Gates points out that 'On a bulletin board, all you have to do is type your message in once and it's available for everybody you want to reach'.[7] Never before has the scope to talk to the world—the whole world—been so accessible. David Lochhead says, 'everyone can have a web page, can tell their own story, promote their own version of the truth for all the world to hear'.[8] The ongoing communications revolution will offer the rising generations access to an unprecedented store of information, and to unimagined communications opportunities—as far beyond print as an ocean is beyond a glass of water. How might this change their perceptions of truth and the value of words—and of books?

2. Speed and transience

An unexpected spin-off of the communications revolution has been an increase to unprecedented levels in the global consumption of printing ink and paper. With cheap printers, easy-to-use software and a torrential throughput of information, homes and offices are printing like never before. But what they publish may not last very long. Where the hard work of producing books afforded them protected status, the ease of printing information is now having the reverse effect. Information is disposable, transient, out of date within hours. You can print it, but somehow the act of printing no longer confers authority—the rarity and mystique are gone. There is a flow to electronic information—it's not static any more.

> Print was designed to convey fact—solid, stable fact. Print could hold a proposition, freeze it so that it could be studied,

dissected, verified. The electronic media were designed to convey news, information that moved so quickly that by the time it could be confirmed or denied, it was no longer news.[9]

How might the rising generations, skilled in dealing with information which is fluid and transient, deal with questions of universal or long-term meaning?

3. Multiplicity and diversity

The term multi-media is now much used and abused, but it does describe one of the most salient features of electronic communication: its capacity to blend and mix image, text and sound in the service of a given message. Marshall McLuhan claims that the electronic media render words 'tactile'—open to being grasped as much by the senses as by the intellect.[10]

By the turn of the millennium, Bill Gates has predicted 'a significant percentage of documents . . . won't be fully printable on paper. You'll still be able to print out a two-dimensional view, but that will be like reading a music score instead of listening to a recording.'[11] Already, according to advertising executive Jim Carroll, 'young consumers are more visually articulate . . . more adept at handling visual ideas'.[12] Neville Brody, the art director behind the revolutionary *Face* magazine, explains further, 'The way we absorb information changes: with digital technology and interactive cable our behaviour is totally different from the past in the way we read text and images, the way we experience visual language.'[13]

Designer Auriea Harvey pushes the very boundaries of multi-media as an Internet artist. Her web-site[14] has won numerous awards and is cited in several books on site design. 'With text everyone feels they "know" what you are saying,' she says: '. . . with images it is left more to interpretation.'[15]

She recognises that this is not just an extension of existing media, but a whole new way of working. 'It took years for me to learn to paint. I imagine the web will take equally as long to become a real means of expression to me.'[16]

Adapting to this multiplicity of information sources, young people are fast becoming 'mosaic thinkers', able to 'integrate disparate information into new perspectives on reality'.[17] They are quickly losing the memory of mono-media communication, and are comfortable with the multi-sensory. Presented with a range of simultaneous sources—image, text, voice, sound, movement—they will take threads from each and weave them into meanings, often in patterns that don't exist in any one of the source 'tracks'. They are able 'to put information together in new patterns, often arriving at unusual, novel, or surprising conclusions'.[18]

The more accustomed young people become to multi-media, the more necessary it will be for a given message to be reinforced through more than one voice. Mono-media communication can quickly appear one-dimensional and uninspiring compared to this 'total experience that is brighter, louder and larger than life itself'.[19] It is not in the script, the image or the music that contact is made, but in the collusion of all three. There is a remarkable new area of communication opening up in random, unpredicted connections—a computer graphic left to make its own connection with the music; the soundtrack from one film played over the images of another; speech, image and rhythm brought together in unrehearsed symphony. In such experiences, the message is discovered rather than dispatched, and is as much to do with intuition as intellect. Dance culture thrives on this randomness, as DJs search for new connections of beat and melody and dancers find their own rhythmic space within them. Multi-media communication, like a net or a web, finds its strength not in strings but in knots—it is the intersections that matter most. But how quickly will those of us used to text and voice learn to handle the new language of multi-media? It's one thing to juggle with one or two information sources—what skills will we need to keep eight in the air?

4. Interaction and response

Alongside multi-media capabilities it is the interactivity of the new communication which marks its departure from the linear, pre-determined nature of traditional text. In print the power to set meanings belongs not to the receiver but to the sender. Electronic and image-based communications, by contrast, invite the receiver to share in the task of creating the message. As young people grow increasingly accustomed to this invitation, they become resistant to messages in which they have no such co-creative role.

The new medium of CD-Rom can combine 'music, graphics, animation and video clips to create a new level of multimedia interactivity'.[20] Mike Large, director of operations for producers Real World, gives an excellent definition of interactive communication in describing Peter Gabriel's project Eve. He explains that Gabriel 'has always wanted his audience to experience his work from the inside, rather than being passive observers or listeners . . . The disc will enable the users to transform and create their own versions of the images and music as they explore the world that has been created'.[21] This 'option expansion' is not the only aspect of the new media which is interactive—there is also the very real sense in which the net is drawing people into increased interaction in 'cyber-communities'. Douglas Rushkoff insists that this, rather than machine-driven interaction, is the real thing. 'Interactivity does not mean interacting with a machine,' he says, 'however real it might feel . . . I suggest that interaction with machines, however temporarily novel, will reveal itself as a poor substitute for using machines to interact with one another'.[22] The Internet provides for the possibility of living 'not in an information age; (but) in an interactive one',[23] in which the new media are simply the devices through which we communicate with other living beings. 'To me the internet is teeming with life, buzzing with thought,' he says. '... All of this terrific spirit, however, comes from us. We are the life coursing through our datasphere's veins.'[24] For Rushkoff and the many co-cyberians who have made this strange new world their home, interactivity is the sum and substance of the net. It is not simply a new means for advertisers to get products into our homes, but a genuine opportunity to multiply human interchange. Communication is the essence of community, and whether interaction lies in the options offered by a CD Rom, or in the interconnectedness of the net, it restores the possibility of response to much of our communicating. There can be no doubt that it will bring deep and lasting changes to our culture.

Capacity and scope; speed and transience; multiplicity and diversity; interaction and response—already these characteristics of post-literate communications are making a difference in the lives of the transitional generations. Some of more significant implications of this are:

The demystifying of authority

Douglas Rushkoff has written extensively on the power of cyberian technology to demystify the 'magic box' of television, taking away its almost priestly power. 'If you're actually moving around the pixels yourself on the screen, you no longer see television as the mystical act,' he says. 'You don't see it as the gospel truth being pumped into your home.' [25] David Lochhead sees the same process attacking the authority of text. 'Text can carry a sense of authority because it is "given",' he says. 'The printed text is solid, unchanging, real . . . With the computer, the text is always tentative . . . In this medium, I control the text. The text does not control me.'[26] Media which for generations have enjoyed priestly status are being stripped of their privileges and left to stand naked.

The reinvention of writing

Jay David Bolter describes the computer as 'a new writing surface that needs conventions different from those of the printed page'.[27] Hypertext, increasingly replacing text as the standard means of writing on a computer, allows the reader to determine where the beginning, middle and end of a piece will lie, plotting their own path of clicks and links through the textual landscape. American author Bob Arellano's novel @ltamont, published on CD-Rom, offers two beginnings. Readers who click on 'Innocence' read about a young couple's first kiss; those who click on 'Experience' read about a murder.[28] Such novels are, in sales terms, a minority interest, but as the influence of the Internet grows, Bolter says, 'Sedate rows of linear text are becoming the exception rather than the rule.'[29] Writing has been at the heart of our notion of civilisation for centuries, and computers are changing the way we write. 'What needs to be clear,' David Lochhead warns, 'is that digital text is *not* print. Our relation to text in a digital culture will be very different to the relation that was created by print technology.' Not only are the new media adding a whole range of information sources alongside text, they are transforming the way we deal with text itself.

The redefining of the book

Charles Handy, among others, has been quick to point out that the electronic media are transforming, rather than displacing, the book.

> The telecommunications revolution will add to the ways we get and pass information—it won't replace them. They said that television would make books unnecessary, but instead we found the television actually bred books, sending people off to read *Pride and Prejudice* who would not previously have dreamt of reading it for pleasure.[30]

Early evidence of the effects of the Internet confirm this: the easy access and searchable databases of on-line bookshops are already leading to a mini-revival in sales from publishers' backlists. 'Just when it appears that a new medium is going to replace its predecessor,' Douglas Rushkoff has said, 'we tend to figure out the true value of the older.'[31]

A helpful analogy might be that of horse-riding. When the internal combustion engine replaced horses as the best means of getting from A to B, that didn't mean the end of human interest in horses. Far from it. Relieved of the drudgery of pulling carts, horses were seen to possess grace, strength and beauty, and the activities which emphasised these qualities grew. Blacksmiths lost jobs, but the racing, show-jumping, trekking and weekend riding industries thrived. It is quite possible that the post-literate future will usher in a golden age of literature, as the book is released from its tedious duty as conveyor of information to become an object of pleasure.

> A book has totemic value. Like a photograph or a piece of jewellery, the impression of ink on paper creates physical connection with its author . . . Computers and the Internet may have taught or at least reminded us of the special ability of books to provide a kind of experience you can't get anywhere else.[32]

New technologies of information retrieval, such as MIT's proposed 'Electronic Ink', may well render the binding and glue of current technology redundant—but it is likely that the book itself, as an object of beauty and pleasure, will remain. In the meantime, just as the capacity of engines is still measured in horsepower, so electronic communications will continue to borrow the language of, 'pages', 'publishing' and 'typefaces'. But don't be fooled by the continuance of terminology—the new forms of communication opening to us will be as different from the printing of books as driving a Mercedes 'S' Class is from riding a donkey. 'If it's in a book, it must be true' will mean nothing to the rising generations of century 21.

The re-evaluation of oral traditions

The speed with which print came to dominate our culture centuries ago meant that skills associated with oral communication were quickly lost. Centuries earlier, Plato had used the character of the King of Egypt to ask whether the invention of writing itself would 'produce forgetfulness in the minds of those who learn to use it , because they will not practise their memory. Their trust in writing, produced by external characters which are no part of themselves, will discourage the use of their own memory within them.'[33] To the skills of memory, self-expression and story-telling kept alive by the oral tradition, Gutenberg's movable type dealt the final death blow that the King of Egypt had feared. But the transition we are now seeing includes, according to Stephen Toulmin, a shift 'from the written to the oral, from the universal to the particular, from the general to the local and from the timeless to the timely'.[34] Delivered from the illusion that printed text is the all-in-all of communication, young people are rediscovering the power of the oral tradition. Perhaps the single most potent sign of this rediscovery lies in the explosive growth of non-celebrity TV chat-shows. With presenters such as Oprah Winfrey, Rikky Lake and Jerri Springer becoming multi-millionaires, there is a never-ending stream, it seems, of ordinary people willing to 'tell their story' on global TV—and millions like them clamouring to watch.

The reordering of social skills

In the age of print, society's glittering prizes were awarded to those adept at handling text. Now, as Colin Morris has said, 'for the first time in five hundred years those groups and professions in society who live by mastery of the spoken and written word no longer dominate our culture'.[35] In their place, a new range of skills will create a new range of skill-bearers. Some of these will be developments from existing vocations—artists become cyber-artists, musicians producing CD-Roms, but there will also be entirely new social functions.

One of these will be the 'information filter'—the communicator who is able to dive deep into the information ocean to bring up the treasures relevant to a given social group. Weekly and monthly magazines are increasingly fulfilling this function. This is a new kind of bucket or barrel—needed not because information is in short supply, but because there is too much of it to process or control. An indication of the sheer scale of the task is given by the early developments in software 'censorship' packages, designed to filter out selected material on the Internet. According to a report by *The Independent* newspaper, 'the US market for filtering software was worth more than $14m in 1997'.[36] The *CyberNOT* list, used by the market-leading package *Cyber Patrol*, includes a staggering 4.5 million banned websites.[37] Functioning in terms of quantity, quality and consumer preference, information filters will be in great demand in the coming years.

The reimagining of education

Terence Ryan, of the 21st Century Learning Initiative, has written extensively of the impact of pre-digital technologies on education. *'Education has been modelled on the work paradigm of mass production,'* he says *'... throughout this century in industrialised nations the management practices of factories have been directly applied to the management of children's learning in schools.'*[38] A linear, deterministic understanding of text has fostered learning in its own image. Digital technology's introduction of new paradigms both for management and for communication are set to dramatically change this picture.

According to John Abbot, Director of the Initiative, 'The emerging, multi-layered knowledge economy ... requires creativity, flexibility, collaboration and the practical skills of the entrepreneur ... Learning has to be about more than schooling.'[39] In the knowledge society, Peter Drucker tells us, 'increasingly, an educated person will be somebody who has learned how to learn.'[40]

Professor of Education Gunther Kress, author of *Before Writing: Rethinking Paths to Literacy,* questions the emphasis on reading skills in a world moving swiftly into post-literacy.

What preparation does the highly traditional literacy agenda that dominates the public debate provide for the demands of that new world? There are things that images can do which writing cannot, and these things will be central to an economy built on the management of vast amounts of information.[41]

Professor Kress offers a detailed analysis of education in transition:

> The new economy demands new kinds of thinking, dispositions to flexibility and innovativeness, new kinds of hand/eye/brain co-ordination and visual analysis of quite extraordinary complexity; kinds of intelligence quite unlike those of the "sedentary skills of reading and writing".[42]

The post-literate world will revolutionise the way we learn, not just in formal education, but as a life-long activity in a world of continuous change.

The requirement for moral judgements

The new cultural landscapes of cyberia will present their inhabitants with new and unfamiliar moral choices. Already electronic communications are bringing out both the worst and the best in human interaction. Relationships have grown from Internet contacts, leading to life-long friendships and marriage. But the Unabomber attack in Oklahoma was also said to have been aided by bomb-making information on the net. 'Today the darkest of dark thoughts can be revealed anonymously in cyberspace', Patrick Dixon warns, 'with pointers for people of like mind to get in touch via e-mail.'[43] The challenge to create morally acceptable norms for cyberculture is immense. According to Bill Buxton of the Toronto Telepresence project,

> The first step is to recognise that this is not a story about technology, nor are the associated issues primarily ones for engineers, technologists or business. Rather it is a story about people and communities. The issues are inherently social, and must be discussed as such if we are to avoid having, yet again, the tail of technology wagging the dog of society.[44]

The post-literate future is a very different place to the world we have known. It will turn upside down the parts of our lives which touch on communications. For those whose lives revolve *around* communication, the turmoil will be considerable. This must include the Church, whose activities include learning, interchange and the formation of community, and whose sense of mission drives her members to prioritise communication. It is imperative that we consider the impact of the post-literate revolution on the Christian faith community.

Notes

1 Joel L. Serdlow, 'Information Revolution', *National Geographic*, October 1995, p.5.
2 *Ibid.*
3 *Ibid.*
4 Quoted in David Lochhead, 'Technology and Interpretation: A Footnote to McLuhan, Internet article, http://www.interchg.ube.ca/dml/martin.html First published in *Journal of Theology* (Dayton: United Theological Seminary 1994). Lochhead explains: 'Galaxies are always complex, and so is McLuhan's thesis. The 'Gutenberg Galaxy' consisted of the complex social, intellectual, cultural and indeed spiritual changes that accompanied the introduction of printing in western culture.'
5 *Ibid.*
6 Interview in Joel L. Serdlow, *op. cit.*, p.6.
7 Bill Gates, *op. cit.*
8 David Lochhead, *op. cit.*
9 *Ibid.*
10 *Ibid.*
11 Bill Gates, *op. cit.*
12 Jim Carroll, 'The Treachery of the Word, The Tyranny of

Choice and Other Areas of Interest', paper delivered to the Whitebread Conference on Youth, 1994.

13 Quoted in Jim Carroll, *op. cit.*

14 Auriea Harvey, Entropy8, http://www.entropy8.com

15 Auriea Harvey, interviewed by Jason Cranford Teague for Network, *The Independent*, 22 June 1998.

16 Auriea Harvey, *op. cit.*

17 George Barna, *op. cit.*, p.185.

18 *Ibid.*

19 Alan Macdonald, *Films in Close-Up*, (IVP, 1991) p.13. 'While we are in this state of dream-like consciousness, film reaches us through a unique combination of story, sound and visual energy to provide a total experience that is brighter, louder and larger than life itself.'

20 'Starwave Teams with Real World Multimedia for new Peter Gabriel Interactive CD Rom', press release, 9 March 1995. http://www.starwave.com/text/starwave/pressrel/gabriel.html

21 Mike Large, *op. cit.*

22 Douglas Rushkoff, 'Getting Loud—The Pitfalls of Interactive Style,' Internet article, http://www.levity.com/rushkoff/getloud.htm

23 *Ibid.*

24 Douglas Rushkoff, 'The Sorcerer's Apprentice', Internet article, http://www.levity.com/rushkoff/sorcerer.htm

25 Douglas Rushkoff, 'On Cyberculture' interview for Ziff-Davis Television,   http://www.zdnet.com/zdtv/thesite/0797w1/iview/iview635 jump 3_070197.html

26 David Lochhead, *op. cit.*

27 Jay David Bolter, *Writing Space: The Computer, Hypertext and the History of Writing*, (Erlbaum: Hillsdale, New Jersey 1991). Quoted in Janice R. Walker, 'Reinventing Rhetoric', Internet article, 1997, http://www.cas.usf.edu/english/walker/papers/rhetoric.html

28 Quoted in Joel L. Serdlow, *op. cit.*, p.9.

29 Jay David Bolter, *op. cit.*

30 Charles Handy, 'Meeting the Future With a Friendly Face',

Internet article, http://www.imc.org.uk/ais/sub/bulletin/guru-feb/handy.htm

31 Douglas Rushkoff, 'A Computer Ate My Book: Part One', Internet article, http://www.levity.com/rushkoff/book1.htm

32 *Ibid.*

33 Plato, *Phaedrus,* quoted in Jay David Bolter, *op. cit.*, p.110.

34 Stephen Toulmin, *Cosmopolis: The Hidden Agenda of Modernity*, (Free Press: New York, 1990), pp.186–192. Quoted in Mike Riddell, *op. cit.* p.106.

35 Colin Morris, *God in a Box: Christian Strategy in a Television Age*, (Hodder and Stoughton: London 1984).

36 Joseph Blindloss, 'A Censor in Cyberspace', *The Independent*, 22 June 1998.

37 *Ibid.*

38 Terence Ryan, 'The Changing Economy Information Communication Technology and New Forms of Business Management: What they Could Means for Education Systems.' Paper prepared for the International Conference Media and Education,' Poznan, Poland, April 1998. http://www.21learn.org

39 John Abbot, 'Learning Has to be about More Than Just Schooling', *The Journal of the 21st Century Learning Initiative*, June 1998. http://www.21learn.org

40 Peter F. Drucker, 'The Age of Social Transformation,' *The Atlantic Monthly*, November 1998, pp.53–80.

41 Prof. Gunther Kress, *The Independent*, 11 June, 1998. Professor Kress is Professor of Education in Relation to English at the Institute of Education, London. http://www.ioe.ac.uk/ccs/kress/index.htm

42 *Ibid.*

43 Patrick Dixon, *Internet Statistics—Life in Cyberspace*, web posting, November 1997. Visit Patrick's homepage at http://www.globalchange.com/main.htm

44 Bill Buxton, *Social Planning and Communities Along the 'Information Highway'*, (University of Toronto/Alias Research/Xerox Parc, July 1994).

7

SCREENAGERS IN LOVE
Living with Post-literate Communication

*The Word became flesh, said St John, and the Church has turned
the flesh back into words.*

Tom Wright[1]

*It gets into your system. The music rushes round your head. The
adrenaline courses through your body. Stopping is not an option.
First you're racing to win, then you're fighting to survive. One
moment you're marvelling at how real everything seems, the
next you can't believe the sheer depth and scale of what you're
getting into. No side effects are yet known but the potential is
widespread. With over 300 different ways of getting the bug and
1 in 10 households already affected, no one is immune.*

Advertising copy for the Sony Playstation[2]

In 1993, advertising executive Jim Carroll was involved
in a research project testing reactions to a range of youth-
orientated magazine titles among a select group of opinion-
leading young people.

I threw about twenty magazines on the floor, and asked them
to pick out any they might be interested in. Having allowed
them to peruse the selection for a few minutes, I quizzed one

woman as to the basis for selecting a particular title. She flicked through it in front of me and pointed out that it had a good feel; she remarked on the interesting type, the unconventional camera angles, the creative art direction. She really seemed to have bought into this magazine. And then suddenly she said, "Oh no. Actually I wouldn't buy it. It's all about Indie music and I don't like that kind of stuff." The point of this story is that this young consumer had gone a long way down the road to reaching a verdict on the title *before* she even considered the nature of its verbal content.[3]

What is being described here is an encounter with a *screenager*,[4] a member of a new generation so impacted by the transition to post-literacy that image has already taken precedence over word. Raised on MTV, Windows, the Web and video rentals, screenagers are already making the journey away from the dominance of text. More concerned with their ZIPs than their zits; more interested in pixels than pimples, screenagers are redefining what it means to be young in terms of an information-rich, visual experience. Young people, Carroll claims, have become victims of the 'treachery of the word'. They

have not just been seduced away from the word and text by other forms of communication. The word has actually betrayed them. Young people rarely even bother to raise a sneer any more at the political double talk of "job seeking" . . . corporate heads talking of "re-engineering the workforce" and "rightsizing"; they discard unread the personalised direct mail letters with computer-drawn signatures—the letters that offer us the chance of a lifetime and present us with an alarm clock . . . No wonder young people read less. What do words *mean* any more?[5]

John Drane expresses a similar sentiment in his reflection on his renowned encounter with young people in the aftermath of the Dunblane tragedy.

These youths instinctively expressed their spirituality not through words but through symbols. In recent years I have gradually been moving towards the conclusion that our words are getting in the way of the gospel—that the church is somehow imprisoned in a kind of cognitive captivity which is inhibiting our mission.[6]

Screenagers are uncomfortable with the traditional authority of text but at home with the visual; stimulated by multimedia but bored by words on a page; alive to the interactive but dead to the passive. Clearly, if the Church, whose history is so rich with words, is to engage this generation, she must break free from whatever captivity words, text and the age of print have imposed. In her conversations with the transitional generations, she must understand that they do not see text the way that she has seen it. This will have a range of implications for the Church's ministry to screenage culture:

- It will impact the ways in which screenagers *communicate*—touching on any aspect of the Church's life that involves the transmission of a message, from posters advertising services to one-to-one counselling.
- It will deeply impact the way screenagers absorb information and *learn*—challenging the Church's work in teaching and education.
- It will impact the way screenagers perceive and use *books*—challenging the central role of the Bible in Church life.

So long scriptura?

The last of these questions represents perhaps the most far-reaching challenge, for the Christian faith community, of the post-literate age. Already, approaches to the Bible are among the hottest topics debated by those working at the frontiers of cultural change. The necessity of printing Bibles was mother to Gutenberg's invention, and the Bible has remained the most-reproduced and best-selling book since. 561 years at number one is an impressive record—making the Bible the book of all books—but it also serves to confirm just how closely the Bible and the age of print are tied together.

The challenge is particularly difficult for the Protestant community—and within that sector, for those who hold to 'a high view of Scripture'.

> Protestant interpretation of Scripture has developed hermeneutical traditions that are well suited to the printed medium. Protestantism is not solely the creature of print. That would be to ignore the spiritual dynamics of the Reformation period. Nevertheless, the print medium became a central factor in the shape that the Protestant Reformation eventually took. Classical Protestantism can aptly be described as the spirituality of print.[7]

How will screenagers, newly exiled from the Gutenberg galaxy, treat this 'book of God' that has been so much a part of print culture? Does the end of the age of print signal the end of the Bible's authority? These are real and pertinent questions, which mark the boundaries of the debate raging among the Church's own younger generations.

Scholarship and pragmatism

Within this debate there are two distinct questions which need to be dealt with in different ways. The first is the 'big question' of theology and hermeneutics—'How will the shift to post-literacy change *what we believe about* the

Bible?' It is to this question that systematic theologians are turning—and their task is extraordinarily complex and delicate. An estimate in litres of the blood spilt in Europe in the years of Reformation and Counter-Reformation would be a useful reminder of just how painful such changes can be. My own stance is that I do not feel qualified even to enter the battle arena, let alone proffer conclusions. I am glad to know that this debate is taking place, and I dare to hope that it will come to a bloodless end. Print technology may have dominated the Church for five centuries, but the narratives and texts of the faith have sustained its life for almost twenty. All the same, I would be cautious, here as anywhere, before wading in.

The second question, though, is more practical and invites us all, qualified or not, to join the debate: 'How will the shift to post-literacy change the *way we engage with* the Bible?' If screenagers struggle to engage with *text* , we must not allow this to stop them from engaging with *truth*. In our struggles to relate an age-old faith deep in tradition and history to generations raised on screenage post-literacy, we will need to rediscover the power of God's word *outside of* the power of text. This will demand that the Church recognise and embrace other forms of expression—not so much alternative truths as alternative means by which truth is accessed and understood. According to Amos Wilder, the Church has always appropriated the communication methods of the culture in which it finds itself, beginning with the very basics of speech.

> Every step of the way, beginning with Jesus himself, represents an identification with and renewal of existing idioms. In one sense, as language, the Gospel met every man and each people where they were—was "all things to all men"—in another sense it spoke a new word to all.[8]

Is it time for an 'identification with and renewal of' the media and idioms of the screenage? If so, some of the places we might start are:

Recovering the power of story

A capitalist was walking one afternoon on the beach at Naples, and was shocked to find a fisherman sitting idly by his boat smoking his pipe.

'Why aren't you out fishing?' the capitalist asked.

'Why should I be?' said the fisherman.

'Well, if you fished all day instead of just the morning' the capitalist explained, 'you would catch more. More fish would mean more profit. You could trade this old boat for something better, buy new nets for even more fish and even more profit. Very soon you could afford to employ a crew to do the work for you.'

'And what would I do then?'

'Then,' said the capitalist triumphantly, 'you could afford to take it easy. You would have time to yourself; you could enjoy the fruits of your labours.'

'And what,' asked the patient old fisherman, 'do you think I'm doing now?'[9]

There is power in story, and the Bible is, as Mike Riddell points out, 'the repository of stories . . . from generations of people who have tried to follow God. It is also the bearer of "the story of all stories": the life and teaching of Jesus . . . the Bible keeps alive for us "the dangerous memory of Jesus".'[10] There is wide support for a re-emphasis at this time on story—a medium founded not in text but in the pre-literacy of oral cultures. David Hillborn has said recently, 'if narrative is the way to communicate to an audience which no longer thinks rationalistically, then preaching will need to change.'[11] Brian Walsh and Richard Middleton insist, 'It is imperative that the Church unequivocally reclaim the

Bible as narrative.'[12] . The truth of story is arrived at in a very different way from that of print. 'Listening to or reading stories is not primarily an application of intellect,' Mike Riddell has said. 'It is an act of shared imagination. In story, one is invited (not coerced) into a different world through the use of active imagining.'[13] Leslie Newbiggin is careful to contrast the eternal significance of the story of God with the transient attempts we make to capture it in text.

> Our so-called eternal truths are the attempts we make at particular moments in the story to grasp and state how things are in terms of our experience at that point. They are all provisional and relative to time and place, as we recognise when as twentieth-century people we read the seventeenth-century language of the Westminster Confession. The reality with which we have to deal is the story—the story that begins before the creation of the world, ends beyond the end of the world, and leads through the narrow road that is marked by the names of Abraham, Isaac and Jacob, Moses, Amos, Paul, and, name above every name, Jesus.[14]

By retaining ambiguity, flexibility and nuance, story delivers us from at least some of the 'cognitive captivity' of text—and at the same time resonates with the new-found agility and interaction of hypertext. Story is fast becoming the common thread running through the many media of the our age. Video games are weak on text but strong on story; advertising increasingly sees its task as selling the product by telling the story; TV, film and video are built on plot above all else; song-writing is in itself a form of storytelling; journalists 'tell the story' where they used to 'print the facts'. In a silent revolution, narrative is replacing print as the unifying element of our culture.

Leighton Ford has argued for a complete transformation of evangelism from outreach built on a rational defence of the gospel's credibility to 'narrative evangelism'—the telling of God's story and its impact on our stories. There is something in the power of story that resonates deeply with a post-literate culture, freeing words to express the full range of their playfulness and charm. 'Anything worth knowing always has a beginning, a middle and an end,' Mike Riddell reminds us, 'and sometimes it takes a while to get from one to the other.'[15] The good news, for the Christian faith community, is that much of the Bible was story before it was anything else—and that the founder of the faith was without doubt one of history's best story-tellers. Christian Scripture is rich with living, colourful, multi-layered stories to fund our culture's imagination. As Walter Brueggemann says, 'perhaps it will help if we give up thinking of it as a "book" and regard it as a "tradition" that continues to be alive and surging among us.'[16]

Recovering a symbolic and visual vocabulary

For John Drane's mourning teenagers, sixteen candles were images of hope; a knife laid down was a symbol of repentance. A culture starved of the potency of image and symbol—robbed of the sensual in the realm of faith—is rediscovering, in the screenage years, their power. David Bosch explains: '*Metaphor, symbol, ritual, sign and myth, long maligned by those interested only in "exact" expressions of rationality, are today being rehabilitated . . . they not only touch the mind and its conceptions, and evoke action with a purpose, but compel the heart.*'[17] From the physical presence of objects, through the symbolic enactment of aspects of faith to the evident power of video and film, screenagers have a vocabulary of worship that takes in more, by far, than words.

For some, the most potent contemporary use of this vocabulary has been seen in the concerts of U2. Bobby Maddex describes the Zoo TV experience: 'Trabant cars hung from the upper rafters of the stage, illuminating a bank of television sets and video screens which flashed random words and phrases (PANIC, SEX, NO ANSWERS, EVERYTHING YOU KNOW IS WRONG) at high speed intervals'[18] For U2, even text is just another image, ripped out of its context and stripped of linear meaning. Meanwhile, back at church, ZOO TV has proved an inspiration to a wave of 'alternative' worshippers, who agree with record-producer T Bone Burnett's assessment: '*A U2 concert is what church should be*'[19] Banked TV sets, video and slide projection, computer graphics and graffiti walls are taking the place of the pulpit as the places in which ideas about God are explored. For pioneers in this field, the management of a worship event is being superseded by the creation of a worship environment: a three-dimensional, multi-media sacred space; a temple made neither of stone nor of words, but of sound and image.

Guided by intuition and the deep longings of the soul, screenagers navigate the many signals of this print-free world, weaving truth from its many threads. Even the Bible itself is to be freed from the cognitive captivity of words to harness the power of image. Jeff Anderson and Mike Maddox have worked for five years to create *The Lion Graphic Bible* (Lion: Oxford, 1998), presenting the whole span of biblical narrative in graphic novel form. Graphic novels—full-length comics to the uninitiated—are more usually the territory of Judge Dredd, Spawn and The Forever People. But the Bible, say Lion, 'is a unique tale of origins and cosmic powers; of the ageless battle between good and evil; of human potential and human treachery; and of a Messiah—a saviour for the world. This is indeed the stuff that graphic

novels are made of.'[20] The power of a single, painted image
is explored in the late Henri Nouwen's remarkable book
The Return of the Prodigal Son.[21] This extended meditation
on the meaning of the famous parable was inspired not by
the text itself, but by Rembrandt's painting of the same
name.[22] Nouwen describes how a chance encounter with a
print of this great masterpiece spoke powerfully to him of
God's love and of his need. He was later able to view the
painting itself in St Petersburg, and he stood for hours
before it, transfixed by the picture and by the truth it carried. The result is a profound and moving exploration of the
story. Image is as varied and as valid a vehicle as text for
communicating truth—and quite possibly a more useful
one in the visual jungle of the screenage years.

Recovering the language of community

Leslie Newbiggin reminds us that the Church 'lives in the
midst of history as a sign, instrument and foretaste of the
reign of God'.[23] Is there a language of community that can
speak to young people resistant to the language of text?
'Truth is not a product, to be processed and packaged and
dispensed.' says Mike Riddell. 'It is an encounter which takes
place when people share their stories in a place of safety and
dignity.'[24] There is mounting evidence that screenagers will
be drawn to 'the places of safety and dignity.' In a world of
dysfunctional relationships, a glimpse of true community
will communicate more than volumes of static prose. 'The
emerging culture is more interested in reality than truth . . .
where there is consistency between word and action.'[25]
David Hillborn sees this as nothing more or less than God's
own preferred way of communicating: 'Just as the divine
Word was embodied in Jesus, so godly words are meant to
be embodied—within relationships and communities of
faith.'[26] Community puts words into actions. Are there

actions we can take—for justice, for the poor, for our neighbours—that to screenagers will be more rich with meaning
than the many words of the Westminster Confession?

Recovering the silence of contemplation

Is it possible that beyond the walls of words that we have
built there lies the possibility of a richer experience of God?
Maggie Dawn suggests that this is so.

> My argument is that the heart of Christian experience is
> engagement not with words but with The Word—God as tran-
> scendent, but met in incarnation . . . we are creatures for whom
> language is a necessary part of making real in our experience
> what we believe to exist in transcendence.[27]

The screenage hunger for experience goes beyond the occa-
sional, intense feelings aroused by acts of corporate worship.
It is the longing for God day by day. Canadian theologian
Ronald Rolheiser calls this 'the eclipse of contemplation'.
'Today we, the children of Western culture . . . struggle with
practical atheism,' he says. 'Our churches are slowly empty-
ing and, more and more, the sense of God is slipping from
our ordinary lives.' The answer, he claims, is not connected to
more words, nor to a better grasp of textual truth. 'The road
back to a lively faith is not a question of finding the right
answers, but of living in a certain way, contemplatively. The
existence of God, like the air we breathe, need not be proven.
It is more a question of developing good lungs to meet it cor-
rectly.'[28] Contemplation taps into two sources of the richness
of God—the power of silence to move us beyond words and
the power of ordinary experience to enlighten us. In both, it
is possible to hear God speak without text. A new generation is rediscovering the insights of such spiritual directors
as the eighteenth-century Jean-Pierre de Caussade, who

could say, even as print was charting its steady course to world domination:

> It is right that we should worship and acknowledge the pro-found wisdom of God. But what is he telling us, in the words he pronounces moment by moment, whose substance is not ink and paper, but what we do and suffer from one moment to the next, do not these deserve our attention? . . . if we read the word of God in the Scriptures through the eyes of faith, it must be wrong to read his works with any other eyes.[29]

Perhaps a generation struggling with text will be better able to read these 'works of God', in the language of human experience. To do so would take God out of the box that we have called religion, and release him into the currency of everyday life—in the heart of a culture desperate for depth. This is the God who is, in the words of Dietrich Bonhoeffer, 'the "beyond" in the midst of our life'. Might it not be in non-verbal experience that a generation disillusioned with text, jaded with too many words, will find fresh faith?

Pentecost in the cacophony

Story, image, community and contemplation—these are four of the weapons in our armoury as we live, pray, worship and communicate in a culture retreating from the high ground of literacy. Our prayer must be that post-literacy will not lead to a disengagement but to a re-engagement with the truths that have brought the Church to its two thousandth year. There is a harsh side to this transition—it will cost the Church the privileged status afforded to it in the Gutenberg galaxy. 'For the first time in the history of Christianity,' Colin Morris has said, 'the Gospel will have to take its chance in the ultimate open society.'[30] The task that faces us is to maintain a voice for the Christian community within the multiplicity and plurality of screenage culture. For David Lochhead, this redefines the priorities of Christian mission. 'In a world of multiple voices,' he asserts, 'the Christian response of witness is one of pointing to and naming the signs of the Spirit in the multitude of voices. It is the task of discerning the Spirit, of locating Pentecost in the cacophony.'[31]

Post-literate culture will present the Church with both challenge and opportunity. The challenge: to extricate our faith from an over-dependence on text—without killing the patient in the process. The opportunity: to re-access, re-examine, rediscover and re-explore 'the story' in new forms. Our success in facing these issues will be greatly significant to the Church's engagement with screenage culture, and thereby to its fortunes in the century that lies beyond the end of print.

Notes

1 Tom Wright, *The Crown and the Fire* (SPCK: London, 1992, p. 51).
2 Sony Computer Entertainment Inc. http://www.playstation-europe.com
3 Jim Carroll, 'The Treachery of the Word, The Tyranny of Choice and other Areas of interest', paper delivered to the Whitebread Conference on Youth, 1994.
4 The term 'screenager' has its origin, I believe, with Douglas Rushkoff, and describes those raised in the visual environment of MTV, the Internet and video games.
5 Jim Carroll, *op. cit.*
6 John Drane, 'Was God in Dunblane?', *Baptist Times*, 21 March 1996, p. 8.
7 David Lochhead, 'Technology and Interpretation: A Footnote to McLuhan', Internet article, http:www.interchg.ubc.ca/dml/

martin.html First published in *Journal of Theology* (Dayton Theological Seminary, 1994).

8 Amos Wilder, *Early Christian Rhetoric* (SCM: London, 1964), p. 59, quoted in Colin Morris, *God in a box* (Hodder and Stoughton: London, 1984).

9 A version of this story is quoted by Charles Handy in *The Future of Work* (Blackwells, 1985), another version in Mike Riddell, *Godzone: A Guide to the Travels of the Soul* (Lion, 1992).

10 Mike Riddell, *Threshold of the Future: Reforming the Church in the Post-Christian West* (SPCK: London, 1998), p. 55.

11 David Hillborn, *Picking Up the Pieces: Can Evangelicals Adapt to Contemporary Culture?* (Hodder and Stoughton: London, 1997), p. 167.

12 J. Richard Middleton and Brian J. Walsh, *Truth is stranger than it used to be* (SPCK: London, 1995), p. 69.

13 Mike Riddell, *op. cit.*, p. 137.

14 Leslie Newbiggin, *The Open Secret* (SPCK: London, 1995), p.83.

15 Mike Riddell, alt.spirit@metro.m3 (Lion, 1997).

16 Walter Bruegemann, *The Bible Makes Sense* (St Mary's Press, 1997).

17 David Bosch, *Transforming mission: Paradigm shifts in Theology of Mission* (Orbis: Mary Knoll, 1991), p. 353.

18 Bobby Maddex, 'A God-shaped Hole; can U2 and a new generation of seekers ever fill it?', *Gadfly Magazine*, August 1997, p. 26. Maddex adds, 'You have this whole generation of seekers who, in some cases, have seen church evolve from the symbolism and mystery of the liturgy to the straightforward logic of revivalism (repent or go to hell) to the entertainment of the rock and roll seeker service . . . U2 voice perfectly what it feels like to be a believer in a society where our spiritual and cultural options seem used, limited, worn-out.' (*Ibid.*, p. 4.)

19 T Bone Burnett, quoted in Bobby Maddex, *op. cit.*, p. 27.

20 Press release, Lion Publishing, July 1998 http://www.lion-publishing.co.uk

21 Henri J. M. Nouwen, *The Return of the Prodigal Son, a story of homecoming* (Dartman, Longman and Todd: London, 1992). A resource for small groups, with audio tape selections from the book, notes and questions and ten colour prints of Rembrandt's paintings is available from St Paul's Media Centre, 199 Kensington High Street, London W8 6BA.

22 See http://www.hermitage.ru/en/western/en_rembr_son.htm

23 Leslie Newbiggin, *op. cit.*, p. 110.

24 Mike Riddell, *op. cit.*

25 Mike Riddell, *op. cit.,* p. 113

26 David Hillborn, *op. cit.*, p. 148.

27 Maggie Dawn in Cray et al, *The Post Evangelical Debate* (Triangle: London, 1997), p. 37.

28 Roland Rolheiser, *The Shattered Lantern: Rediscovering a felt presence of God* (Hodder and Stoughton: London, 1994). Rolheiser is a member of the Oblates of Mary Immaculate and has taught theology and spirituality around the world.

29 Jean-Pierre De Caussade, *The Sacrament of the Present Moment*, eighteenth century, trans. Kitty Muggeridge (Fount Paperbacks: London, 1981).

30 Colin Morris, *op. cit.*

31 David Lochhead, *Technology, Communication and the Future*, Internet article, 1995. http://www.interchg.ubc.ca/dml/future.html

8

THIS IS MY TRUTH,
TELL ME YOURS[1]

The Post-modern Worldview

*An epoch approaches its end when its fundamental conviction
begins to weaken and no longer inspires enthusiasm among its
advocates.*

Albert Borgman[2]

*Postmodernism is a contemporary movement. It is strong and
fashionable. Over and above this, it is not altogether clear what
the devil it is.*

Ernest Gellner[3]

In 1967, my family moved to a rented house in Paris. The
intention was that we stay for one academic year. My father
had arranged a sabbatical, and was to work on his PhD
thesis at the Sorbonne. Like the best-laid plans, our inten-
tions were thwarted. Growing tension among both students
and workers in France erupted in the riots of May 1968, in
which thousands took to the streets and fought running
battles with the 'Police National'. We would be given a day
off school if a march was planned in our quartier; we would
walk past burnt-out cars in the street; my father would
come home with his eyes streaming from the tear gas that

had leaked from the Place Montparnasse to the Metro lines below. Eventually the Sorbonne was closed and a general strike gripped the country. Uncomfortable with the prospect either of prolonged chaos or of a communist government, my father packed us into the car and sped us north to the coast and to England—on the last ferry to leave before the strike shut the channel ports down. As we drove across the Pas de Calais at dawn, smokeless factory chimneys could be seen adorned with the Red Flag of the hoped-for revolution. An eerie silence lay across the land as Europe held its breath and all eyes were on France. In the event, the skilled intervention of De Gaulle broke the student-worker alliance and order was restored. Neither my family, nor the thousands of others caught in these events, were aware of the significant role that this crisis would play in the philosophical history of France—and of the world.

To all those involved in them, 'les événements' (the events) of May 1968 remained a deeply etched experience. The revolution never came—in a sense the dream was over—and the years following were marked in France by reflection and re-evaluation by the radical left. If the sixties' 'revolution' had ended in such disarray, if Marxism and modernism alike had failed, where was there to turn to? Out of this disappointment, this search for a new, more permanent radical edge, a new philosophical movement was born. Disillusionment with the sixties' counter-culture created a vacuum in philosophy, and a generation of young French philosophers, not unlike the post-war existentialists before them, stepped in with '*the newest avant-garde in theory and politics, more radical than radical and newer than new; the hyperradical and hypernew*'.[4] This is the movement we now call postmodernism.

The birth of an *ism*

Much of the material from which these young writers constructed their theories had been around for some time, not least in the work of the philosopher Neitzsche. The term post-modern had been in use in the art world from the early part of the century, and a range of ideas challenging the assumptions of modernity had been published over several decades. Many of the changes we now identify with the demise of modernity were well underway by the 1970s, but no one had constructed theories which tied all these things together. As Stephen Connor has said, the 'concept of post-modernism cannot be said to have crystallised until about the mid 1970s'.[5] From this point Jean-Francois Lyotard, Jaques Derrida, Jean Buadrillard and, in America, Richard Rorty published a series of works which have become the classic texts of post-modern theory. In the words of Best and Kellner, these theorists claim that 'in the contemporary high-tech media society, emergent processes of change and transformation are producing a new post-modern society ... the era of postmodernity constitutes a novel state of history and novel sociocultural formation which requires new concepts and theories.'[6] Hundreds of other authors have now joined them with developments, rebuttals, applications and examinations of these theories and the term post-modern is in everyday use.

Speaking in 1946, when existentialism was growing in popularity at a similar rate, Jean-Paul Sartre said:

> Many of those who are making use of this word would be highly confused if required to explain its meaning. For since it has become fashionable, people cheerfully declare that this musician or that painter is 'existentialist'. . . . the word is now

so loosely applied to so many things that it no longer means anything.[7]

Much the same could be said of postmodernism, which has followed its parent to become a 'flavour of the month' philosophy, used to describe an immense range of products and ideas from breakfast TV shows through advertising campaigns to the highest realms of art and academia. Postmodern is becoming a catch-all adjective for anything that is different from the way it was last year. Even among those who use the term fluently, a coherent meaning has not yet emerged. 'There is no unified post-modern theory,' Best and Kellner inform us, 'or even a coherent set of positions. Rather, one is struck by the diversities between theories often lumped together as 'post-modern' and the plurality—often conflictual—of post-modern positions.'[8]

In this confusion, it is important to be aware that postmodern*ity* and postmodern*ism* are not entirely the same. Those who doubt that such similar words can have dissimilar meanings need only consider the significance of the words spirituality and spiritualism. The journey from an *ity* to an *ism* can be long and complex. Broadly, postmodern*ity* is the condition in which we find ourselves as the 'modern' era draws to a close. It is descriptive of a period in history, a cultural ethos at a given time. Postmodern*ism* , on the other hand, is a specific philosophical response to this condition. As Gene Veith has said, 'If the modern era is over, we are all post-modern, even if we reject the tenets of postmodernism.'[9]

This overlap of terminology creates an interplay between the actual: the things that are happening in our culture as modernity ends, and the uttered: the things that are being said about what is happening. Many of the traits of postmodernity that culture-watchers are describing do not stem from the philosophy of postmodernism at all; they are symptomatic of wider historical and social change. At the same time, the speed with which this philosophy has become accepted in the West, especially among the young, demonstrates that for many people what is being said (the *ism*) strongly resonates with what is happening (the *ity*). To put it another way, postmodern*ism* is not the only possible response to postmodern*ity*, but it is a response that rings true for many people.

Definitions

The world of Generation X and beyond will be post-modern in the sense that:

1. The influence of 'modernity' as a central fund of social and philosophical ideas will be greatly lessened.
2. A new group of ideas will come together to form the concepts of 'postmodernity'.
3. Within this process, the theories of postmodernism will play a part as an influential voice in the new paradigm.
4. Evidence for the influences both of postmodernity and of postmodernism will be seen most clearly in the lives of the transitional generations.

As we consider the post-modern nature of the emerging culture, we need to ask ourselves four questions:

1. What is the nature of this modernity that is coming to an end?
2. What are the broad strokes of the emerging condition of postmodernity, influenced as it is by the philosophies of postmodernism?
3. What will the impact of these changes be on the transitional generations?

4. What challenges will this bring for the Christian faith
    community?

As before, the last of these questions will be dealt with in
detail in a separate chapter. The first three will be our concern now. Because it is both a philosophical shift and a
broad social movement, developing and unfolding even as
we try to understand it, postmodernity is a moving target in
a changing field. One way of beginning to understand it is
to capture what it is that we are losing—what this
'modernity' has been about.

Building Babel

A widely-quoted measurement of the modern era is that
given by theologian Thomas Olden, who claims that modernity was born in the storming of the Bastille in the French
revolution of 1789 and lived exactly 200 years to the fall of
the Berlin Wall in 1989.[10] As Gene Veith explains, 'The revolutionaries who installed the 'Goddess of Reason' in Notre
Dame Cathedral ushered in an age of social engineering,
culminating in the grandiose pretensions of Communism . . .
with its totalitarian control of every facet of human life.'[11]

The ideas central to the French Revolution, ideas which
together we now know as the Enlightenment, grew through
the eighteenth century and became the foundational creeds
of modernity. Central to these ideas is the supremacy of
reason, expressed in scientific enquiry and giving birth to
technological progress. 'Modernists genuinely believed that
science would answer all questions,' Veith says, 'and that the
application of scientific principles would solve all social
problems. Through rational planning, applied technology
and social manipulation, experts could engineer the perfect
society.'[12]

Walsh and Middleton compare this process to the building of a Babel-like tower. 'The first or ground floor of the building of modernity was science,' they explain, ' . . . science has laid the foundations of modern progress.' Onto that foundation was built an increasing faith in the products of science—the machines that began to fill our lives as the industrial revolution took hold. 'Technology thus constitutes the second floor in the Western building of progress.' But the building didn't stop with the machines—they were harnessed to produce wealth, so that 'economic growth, seen as the purpose and raison d'être of industrial and scientific progress, became the third floor of the building of Western culture'.[13] The supremacy of reason, the enterprise of science, the toys of technology and the dream of universal prosperity—these are the contours of the modernist worldview: in Bob Goudzwaard's memorable term, the 'idols of our time'.

What was envisioned by modernists, Walsh and Middleton explain, was:

> A veritable utopia of prosperity and progress in which the whole human race would be united . . . Human progress is not only possible but inevitable, we have come to believe, if only we allow autonomous reason the freedom to investigate our world scientifically. By this free and open investigation . . . humanity will be able to acquire the technological power necessary to control nature and bring about the ultimate human goal: increased economic consumption and affluence, with resulting peace, fulfilment and security.[14]

The impact of this vision not only on our culture but on its churches is summed up by Tom Sine in the chilling words, *'We have sold our young the wrong dream.'*[15]

The real world strikes back

So what happened? How did the vision of the enlighten-ment—which has given us so much in terms of technology, prosperity, leisure and progress—lose its magnetic force, its power to inspire our lives? The answer, simply put, is that reality stepped in. 'After slavery, two world wars, commu-nism, nazism and nuclear bombs,' says D. Martin Fields 'people began to question the belief that the pursuit of reason, technology and science would make for a better world.'[16] Walsh and Middleton see the genesis of this despair in the existentialism of post-war Europe, when:

> Existentialist writers, whether Christian or atheist, articulated in novels, plays, essays and assorted philosophical writings a profound loss of hope and sense of angst (undefined anxiety or dread) about the meaning and purpose of life in modern times. In this they became the precursors of our contemporary post-modern consciousness.[17]

Not long after this a countercultural movement exploded across the West, giving voice to this same existential angst. 'The counterculture of the 1960s began looking for some-thing different,' says Veith 'and in many ways its advocates were the pioneers of postmodernism. As the student pro-testors grew up, they entered academia, the professions and the mainstream of the culture, bringing their "new con-sciousness" with them.' This brings us full circle to Paris in 1968, and the founding voices of post-modern theory. 'Scholars began submitting scientific rationalism to a withering critique,' Veith continues, 'arguing that what is presented as objective truth is often a mask for personal bias, cultural prejudice and power politics.'[18] If it is nothing else, then, postmodernity is a critical reaction to modernity.

Christopher Jones, of St Peter's College, Oxford, has written, 'It is perhaps best to see postmodernism as a corrective to the excesses of modernity, and a purgative to its pathologies.'[19] Postmodernists are working hard to articulate a proactive philosophy—but there can be no doubt that postmodernity, at its root, is reactive. 'First,' Jones writes, 'postmodernism defines itself negatively against the universal principles of knowledge and conduct characteristic of the period since the European enlightenment.' Dave Tomlinson puts the same view in the form of a question. 'What happens,' he asks, 'when the modern world loses its romance? When dreams of progress for the common good of humankind turn into nightmares like Bosnia and Rwanda?'[20] The answer is that postmodernity happens.

Into the hall of mirrors

What then is postmodernity? What are the contours of the culture that is emerging in place of the brash optimism of the modern progress-myth? To answer this question is to piece together clues from a vast range of sources. It is like searching a crowd by the light of a mirror-ball: fragmented spots of light are hitting disparate and unconnected corners of the culture. In my own exploration of these themes, I have been greatly helped by the work of a number of Christian scholars, including Stanley J. Grenz, Middleton and Walsh and Gene Veith, and by the insightful summaries of postmodernity offered by Mike Riddell and David Hillborn. What follows is an amalgamation of these and other sources, tempered by my own anecdotal experience of working with young people on the voyage to the planet postmodernity. Theirs is a complex, multiple journey, and in our attempts to understand it, I believe it essential that we address five tensions or conflicts inherent in the modern vs post-modern transition.

1. Dogma vs deconstruction

The most famous attempt at self-definition made by a post-modernist is that of Jean-Francois Lyotard: 'Simplifying in the extreme, I define post-modern as incredulity toward metanarratives.'[21] The failure of modernity, Lyotard is saying, has left Western culture suspicious not only of the big story of science-and-progress myth, but of any big story that sets itself up as the answer to the whole of life. Meta-narratives, according to post-modern scholar Patricia Waugh, are 'Large-scale theoretical interpretations pur-portedly of universal application'.[22] Veith sees the failure of modernity as more than a simple questioning of science: 'The bitterness of its critics suggests not mere disillusion-ment but, more deeply, loss of faith. Modernism, in effect, failed as a religion.'[23] Burned by the betrayal of modernity, postmodernists are determined to reject every 'story' that claims to be 'THE story'—such claims, they say become 'totalising' and inevitably lead to the marginalisation and oppression of other stories. They want, in the words of Mike Riddell, 'to throw the doors open and listen to all the stories',[24] to bring the margins into the centre. Thus truth is neither absolute nor abstract—it can exist only as the 'indwelt truth' of local stories. There is no limit to the num-ber of possible stories, and there is no basis on which to assign them anything but equal worth. As the College De France report on education summarised, 'Today there is no more truth or falsehood, no stereotype or innovation, no beauty or ugliness, but only an infinite array of pleasures, all different and all equal.'[25] Richard Rorty captures the scale of this climb-down from meta-narrative in his definition of objectivity as 'agreement amongst everyone who is in the room at the time'.[26]

History, for postmodernists, is a series of metaphors rather than an account of things that actually happened, and since every story carries the corrupting perspective of its author, all texts and truths must be 'deconstructed':

> A mode of analysis that purports to take apart all expressions of objective meaning, showing that everything from a play by Shakespeare to the Declaration of Independence to a scientific experiment is actually unstable linguistic constructions, masks for cultural power and rationalisations for oppression.[27]

These two factors—the rejection of metanarrative and the deconstruction of all truth-claims—are the closest thing post-modernists have to a core creed. They form a rock-solid floor to the new building of postmodernity. From them come some of the most significant characteristics of the emerging age, an age in which:

- *open-ended pluralism* replaces the *assumed superiority* of any single idea or creed;
- *ambiguity* replaces *certainty* and *ambivalence* takes the place of *faith*;
- *coherent systems of meaning* are rejected, to be replaced by *fragmented mosaic patterns.*

Survival in this jungle depends on three simple rules: trust no one, suspect everyone, take nothing at face value. Above all, reject anyone who claims to bring you a truth that might claim to be THE truth. Rejecting meta-narrative presents the emerging culture with a significant dilemma. It is, quite rightly, anti-totalising, and appeals to a generation 'cynical of a concept of truth which has been defined by a small group of "experts" (white, male, European academics), and used to dominate and silence any other voices in the community'.[28] But it is also directionless, offering no framework to function 'as a navigational guide throughout life'.[29] If there is no moral order other than that which we each impose on our own 'constructed' world, then the world 'is devoid of meaning; it is a universe of nihilism where theories float in a void, unanchored in any secure harbour'.[30] In such a universe, 'The experience of the world as our "home", in the sense of a place where we know the rules and responsibilities of the house, is lost and a nomadic homelessness dominates the ethical horizon.'[31] A post-modern generation is a generation a long way from home, confused and wandering. A generation that has lost the map, and is fast losing the will to look for it again.

2. Reason vs intuition

If the enthronement of reason in 1789 was the central act of modernity's birth, then the shift to postmodernity will raise questions about the place of reason in our lives. And if reason and logic are no longer the doorkeepers of experience, a post-modern generation will want to open and explore other, neglected, ways of knowing. 'The post-modern framework,' Kevin Ford says, 'allows for the existence of realities that science cannot measure—the supernatural, the transrational, the spiritual, the eternal, the ineffable, the numinous.'[32] Those growing up in this new post-rational culture will show a greater openness to ideas presented in non-rational forms and to experiences rooted in non-empirical reality. The defined certainties of systematic thinking are thrown over for the ambiguity of story. Linear and rational argument gives way to juxtaposition, sampling and collage, allowing for 'intuitive leaps of meaning'.[33] A shift in music from melody to rhythm as the heart of the enterprise is indicative of this change. Feelings are back on the agenda; 'dignity is granted to emotions and intuition.'[34] The rational man of modernity who did not need to trust in anything beyond logic and sensory experience no longer dominates. Postmodern man is in the house. 'With the demise of the absoluteness of human reason and science,' D. Martin Fields has written, 'the super-natural, that which is not empirical, is once again open to consideration.'[35] The rejection of an unseen world beyond the seen is losing its strength in our culture; belief in spiritual forces is no longer considered antithetical to an intelligent worldview. As Walter James and Brian Russel have said, 'The suspicion of and distaste for the exclusively rational leads in some measure to a re-enchantment of the world, reducing the tendency to treat wonders as commodities.'[36] Postmodernity is reopening the doors rationality and empiricism slammed shut. 'The spiritual dimension,' Dave Tomlinson says, 'is once again talked about with great ease.'[37]

3. Progress vs pessimism

The analysis offered by Middleton and Walsh among others is very clear in putting the 'progress myth' at the heart of modernity: if the enlightenment was about nothing else, it was about a better future for humanity. Postmodernity sweeps away any such notion—without a unified vision of what is right or good, there can be no vision of the better future. Stanley J. Grenz writes:

In eschewing the enlightenment myth of inevitable progress, postmodernism replaces the optimism of the last century with a gnawing pessimism. Gone is the belief that every day and in every way, we are getting better and better. Members of the emerging generation are no longer confident that humanity will be able to solve the world's great problems.[38]

No big story means no big finale: we are not heading anywhere in particular and there is no great climax to look forward to. 'The loss of a future which can be constructed and participated in has lasting effects on the way in which people structure their lives,' says Mike Riddell, 'The focus shifts very much to the present, with the emphasis on extracting as much enjoyment out of that sphere as possible, and damn the consequences.'[39] Despair and hedonism; suicide and escape—in reality these are two sides of the same coinage of angst, and postmodernity is providing more and more places to spend it.

4. Creed vs community

If only local narratives have meaning and if the only truth is indwelt truth, a new emphasis will be placed on the search for community. In the modern age, it was the abstract creeds, whether of science or of religion, that held people together; in the post-modern age it will be the inter-relationships of networks, cells, friendships and communities. Relationships are very important to postmodernity, and are measured in organic rather than mechanistic terms. Philosopher Alisdair MacIntyre, though not himself a postmodernist, supports the view that truth and moral guidance can only be found in community. 'I can only answer the question "What am I to do?",' he says, 'if I can answer the prior question "Of what story or stories do I find myself a part?"'[40] Postmodernism's attack on the monolithic institutions of modernity opens the door for their break-up into smaller, more intimate communities, each living out its own 'story'.

Placed against the backdrop of the increasing dysfunctionality of the family in Western society, this search for authentic community will emerge as one of the primary drives and motivations of a post-modern generation.

5. Commitment vs choice and change

Ironically the very philosophical shift that sends postmoderns off in search of community predisposes them NOT to commit once they get there. Removing the power of metanarrative opens the door to such a flood of choice and opportunity that long-term commitments seem unwise: what if something better were to come along tomorrow? 'Experience is a series of unrelated "presents", divorced from ethics and dogma. Nomadic wanderings replace purposeful pilgrimage.'[41] Life is about travelling, not about arriving—today's journey is good for today, but tomorrow another road beckons. If a lifetime's commitment is to emerge, it will do so not as the result of a once-for-all decision, but because of the experiential quality and value of a whole series of decisions linked together. Loyalties are frequently re-evaluated in the light of changing circumstances. Experience, like bread, goes quickly stale. So powerful is the post-modern emphasis on choice and change, that it attacks the one constant, unchanging element at the heart of modernity—the self.

Central to the enlightenment project was the autonomous self. For believers, the self is rooted in the existence of the God who has created it, hence John Calvin's words, 'The true knowledge of ourselves is dependent on the true knowledge of God.' For enlightenment rationalists with no time for such superstitions, the self is *in itself* the centre of the universe, hence Descartes' 'I think therefore I am'. Either way, self-assurance, self-confidence, self-awareness have been strong elements in both belief and unbelief through the modern era. Postmodernism puts an end to such assurance. According to Kenneth Gergen, 'Under post-modern conditions, persons exist in a state of continuous construction and re-construction; it is a world where anything goes that can be negotiated.'[42] If rationalism said 'nothing is sure or certain except the self', postmodernism says 'nothing is sure or certain, not even the self'. The self reinventions of Bono and Madonna are icons of this age, in which the dictum 'if it feels good, do it' has become 'if it feels good be it'. Richard Lints has written that 'Madonna is in many ways a perfect personification of the post-modern reality: sensation without substance, motion without purpose, a self-centred persona undergoing perpetual change for its own sake.'[43] No more able to look into the mirror of a knowable and coherent nature than into the mirror of a known God, we live instead in the hall of mirrors, presented with so many alternative selves that we become 'paralysed in the face of it all'.[44] A post-modern generation will not only be in search of meaning and community—they will be in search of some anchor, some solid point of reference from which they can answer the question, 'Who am I?'

These five conflicts: dogma vs deconstruction, reason vs intuition, progress vs pessimism, creed vs community and commitment vs choice and change mark out the key themes of the transition into postmodernity. For the Christian faith community, they identify a whole range of issues that the coming decades will present us with.

Notes

1 Album title, Manic Street Preachers, 1998, see http://www.manics.easynet.co.uk/index2.htm

2 Albert Borgman, *Crossing the Post-modern Divide* (University of Chicago Press: Chicago, Ill., 1992), p. 48, quoted in J. Richard Middleton and Brian J. Walsh, *Truth is stranger than it used to be* (SPCK: London, 1995), p. 11.

3 Ernst Gellner, *Postmodernism, Reason and Religion* (Routledge: London, 1992), p. 22, quoted in Riddell, *Threshold of the Future* (SPCK: London, 1998), p. 101.

4 Steven Best and Douglas Kellner, *Post-modern Theory—Critical Interrogations* (1991), introduction. Accessed at http://doc.cc.utexas.edu/%7Ekellner/pm/pm.html

5 Stephen Connor, *Postmodernist Culture: An Introduction to Theories of the Contemporary* (Basil Blackwell: Cambridge Ma. 1989), p. 6. quoted in D. Martin Fields, 'Postmodernism', *Premise*, Volume 2, Number 8, September 1995.

6 Steven Best and Douglas Kellner, *op. cit.*

7 Jean-Paul Sartre, *Existentialism and Humanism*, trans. Philip Mairet (Methuen: London, 1948), p. 25

8 Steven Best and Douglas Kellner, *op. cit.*

9 Gene Edward Veith, *Post-modern Times: A Christian Guide to Contemporary Thought and Culture* (Crossway Books: Wheaton, Ill., 1995), p. 42, quoted in D. Martin Fields, *op. cit.*

10 Thomas C. Oden, *Two Worlds: Notes on the Death of Modernity in America and Russia* (IVP: Downers Grove, Ill., (1992), p. 32, quoted in D. Martin Fields, *op. cit.*

11 Gene E. Veith, 'Post-modern Times: Facing a World of New Challenges and Opportunities', *Modern Reformation*, September/October 1995.

12 *Ibid.*

13 J. Richard Middleton and Brian J. Walsh, *op. cit.*, pp. 16–17.

14 *Ibid*, p. 19.

15 Address to Spring Harvest, Minehead, 1997. Sine develops the idea that all human cultures are driven by their vision of 'the preferred future', and that ours is expressed in exclusively economic terms. See *Wild Hope* (Monarch: Crowborough 1992).

16 D. Martin Fields, *op. cit.*

17 J. Richard Middleton and Brian J. Walsh, *op. cit.*, p. 23.

18 Gene E. Veith, *op. cit.*

19 Christopher Jones, The Good, The Bad and Theology, in *Tomorrow is Another Country* (Board of Education of the General Synod of the Church of England: London, 1996), p. 22.

20 Dave Tomlinson, *The Post Evangelical*, (Triangle: London, 1995).

21 Jean-Francois Lyotard, *The Post-modern Condition: A Report on Knowledge*, trans. G. Bennington and B. Massumi (Manchester University Press: Manchester, 1984), quoted in J. Richard Middleton and Brian J. Walsh, *op. cit.*, p. 70.

22 Patricia Waugh, *Postmodernism; A Reader* (Edward Arnold Publishers: London, 1992), p. 1. quoted in D. Martin Fields, *op. cit.*

23 Gene E. Veith, *op. cit.*

24 Mike Riddell, *op. cit.*, p. 105.

25 Colin Gunton, *The One, The Three and The Many: God, Creation and the Culture of Modernity* (Cambridge University Press: Cambridge, 1993), p. 105, quoted in Michael Horton, 'Where Now? Suggestions for the Way Forward', *Premise*, Volume 2, Number 8, September 1995.

26 Walter Brueggemann, *Texts Under Negotiation*, (Fortress: Minneapolis, 1993), p. 8, quoted in Jimmy Long, *Generating Hope: A Strategy for Reaching the Post-modern Generation* (IVP: Downers Grove, Ill., 1997).

27 Gene E. Veith, *op. cit.*

28 Mike Riddell, *op. cit.*, p. 105.

29 J. Richard Middleton and Brian J. Walsh, *op. cit.*, p. 62.

30 Steven Best and Douglas Kellner, *Post-modern Theory— critical interrogations* (1991), p. 127. Available at http://doc.cc.utexas.edu/%7EKellner/pm/pm.html

31 J. Richard Middleton and Brian J. Walsh, *op. cit.*, p. 61.

32 Kevin Ford, *Jesus for a New Generation: Reaching Out to Today's Young Adults* (Hodder and Stoughton: London, 1996), p.122.

33   Mike Riddell, *op. cit.*, p. 105.

34   Dave Tomlinson, *op. cit.*, p. 140.

35   D. Martin Fields, *op. cit.*

36   Walter James and Brian Russel, 'How Has Postmodernism Changed Education?' In *Tomorrow is Another Country*, (Board of Education of the General Synod of the Church of England: London, 1996), p. 32.

37   Dave Tomlinson, *op. cit.*, p. 140.

38   Stanley J. Grenz, *A Primer on Postmodernism* (William B. Erdmans: Grand Rapids, Mi., 1995), p. 7.

39   Mike Riddell, *op. cit.*, p. 109.

40   Alisdair MacIntyre, *After Virtue: A Study in Moral Theory* (University of Notre Dame Press: Notre Dame, 1984), p. 216, quoted in J. Richard Middleton and Brian J. Walsh, *op. cit.*, p. 68.

41   Yvonne Craig, 'What in the World is Happening?', in *Tomorrow is Another Country*, p. 11.

42   Kenneth J. Gergen, *The Saturated Self: Dilemmas of Identity in Contemporary Life* (Basic Books: New York, 1991), p. 7, quoted in J. Richard Middleton and Brian J. Walsh, *op. cit.*, p. 53.

43   Richard Lints, *The Fabric of Theology* (Eerdmans: Grand Rapids, Mi., 1993), p. 216, quoted in Jimmy Long, *op. cit.* It is worth noting that Madonna's latest transition—into motherhood—has by her own admission challenged a self-centred orientation and is leading to a more reflective, 'spiritual' body of work. Evidence perhaps that self-reinvention can move in positive as well as negative directions.

44   From the Bruce Cockburn song 'Gavin's Woodpile', Golden Mountain Music Corporation, 1976, quoted in J. Richard Middleton and Brian J. Walsh, *op. cit.*, p. 55.

9

RE-IMAGINEERING THE CHURCH
Living with the Post-modern Worldview

If Christianity cannot be inculturated successfully within the post-modern context, there will be no Western church.

Graham Cray[1]

How will you reach this post-modern generation—a generation that cannot conceive of objective truth, cannot follow your linear arguments, cannot tolerate anything (including evangelism) that smacks of religious intolerance?

Kevin Ford[2]

There is a memorable scene in the film *Hook*[3] in which the adult Peter Pan, played by Robin Williams, tries to re-enter the imaginary world seen as real by the lost boys. They sit down to a great feast together at which all the food is imaginary. At first Peter sees nothing, but as he slowly recovers the power of imagination a tableful of rich and colourful dishes begins to appear, until the feast descends into the kind of food-fight that only Hollywood can provide. At the crucial moment, when Peter is first able to imagine again, a wide-eyed lost boy looks to him with admiration and excitement, 'You're doing it Peter,' he cries, 'you're imagining.'

For many of those struggling to relate the Christian faith to postmodernity, this is an apt image. The sense is that there is something to be recovered, a richness and colour to the faith that the rationalism and empiricism of modernity has taken from us. The task is not simply to rearrange the furniture in the Church's shop window, but to re-imagine faith in a new context. 'Re-imagination should not be regarded as a superficial marketing ploy,' Nigel Wright has said, 'but as an intellectually serious act of self-definition.'[4]

For the Church, it is important to understand that engagement with postmodern*ity* is not the same as acceptance of postmodern*ism*. Our primary concern, a concern which none of us can afford to evade, must be to understand postmodernity as a description of the times in which we live. The task of re-imagining faith in this new context is incumbent upon us for two reasons, captured in the quotes above from Graham Cray and Kevin Ford. The first is that only a re-imagined Church will *survive* in the West of the twenty-first century The second is that only a re-imagined Church will *appeal* to the generations shaped by the emerging paradigms. Recognising these twin goals, I propose to take each of the five tensions described in Chapter 8 and to look briefly at the issues these raise for the Church. We will do this in the form of a brief list, under each, of suggested action points. As Graham Cray has said, 'The central question to be faced is how should we respond to the emerging culture in a way which is true to the gospel . . . It is through risk and experiment together with the making of mistakes that the future shape of the Church in mission will be established.'[5] What, then, can the Christian community do to prepare itself for a post-modern culture and to embrace those shaped by it?

In the tension of dogma vs deconstruction

Revisit the biblical metanarrative

For Middleton and Walsh, the answer lies in recovering the truth that the biblical metanarrative is 'anti-totalising' in its impact.

> The biblical metanarrative addresses our post-modern situation with both compassion and power. But does this metanarrative escape the post-modern charge of totalisation and violence? On our analysis, it does far more than that. Far from promoting violence, the story the Scriptures tell contains the resources to shatter totalising readings, to convert the reader, to align us with God's purposes of shalom, compassion and justice.[6]

What this will mean in practice is a willingness to hear the multiple stories of postmodernity, and to see the Christian meta-narrative as the means by which God is able to indwell and transform each:

> Postmodernists are right: the voices of the marginalised, of those who have been left outside the storyline that has been dominant in the West, need to be heard . . . But we need to hear anew not so we can appropriate these voices for our own agenda, nor to conspire toward some sort of God's-eye view of the world . . . Rather, we need to be able to hear each other and the whole creation that we might join together in fulfilling the story of redemption.[7]

In this approach, 'becoming a Christian' does not mean stepping out of our own local story into God's global epic; it means allowing God to walk with us in our story. God comes both in affirmation and in judgement of every culture—but he comes incarnate, in humility. Far from squashing every local story into one, he is, in his person, the fulfilment of each one.

Recover biblical humility

Nick Mercer sees the engagement with the post-modern as a reminder of our own limitations, and an opportunity to recover humility. 'There are no more certainties: only reasonable grounds for confidence,' he says 'This must give us a degree of humility in our walk with others of differing theological positions, and in our dealings with those struggling with faith and practice.'[8]

Don't mistake deconstruction for dismissal

Deconstruction is a way of dealing with knowledge and truth claims, a shift in emphasis from uncritical acceptance to critical engagement. For those raised on modernity, it feels more like rejection and dismissal. If I offer you a new Walkman and the first thing you do is open it up to check the works, I may find your suspicions offensive—but if that is how you have been taught to treat all truth claims, I may have to learn to live with it. Those who bring critical deconstruction to the faith are not always doing so in the hope of rejecting or destroying it—many are doing so in the hope that it will stand. As Walter James and Brian Russel urge, 'The Church should welcome and embrace the less authoritarian and more learner-centred styles of education that the post-modern spirit exacts.'[9]

In the battle of reason vs intuition

Make room for non-linear thinking

Traditional, modernist-oriented, evidential apologetics relies on creating a sense of "cognitive dissonance" within the other person—a sense that his or her own belief structure does not logically square with reality. But [this] approach just doesn't cut it any more—not with Generation X . . . With my generation you won't hear "you're right". You'll hear "whatever. . . ."[10]

While in some ways the Church has been at odds with modernity from its inception, in others it has adapted all too well. One of these has been the tendency to present biblical truths in the systematic, linear, rationalistic forms picked up from the sciences. A post-modern generation rejects this approach, and is looking for ambiguity, intuitive scope, emotional resonance. None of these is captured well in 'four spiritual laws'.

Take emotion seriously

Much has been written, in dismissal as well as in support, about the 'therapeutic age' in which we live. For good or ill, where modernity trusted facts and doubted feelings, post-modernity is switching the polarity. For the Church, this is an opportunity to restore balance, and to embrace the biblical wholism that views people—heart, soul, strength and mind—as a unity. The re-imagining of our faith in the post-modern context may offer us the chance to heal old wounds, re-uniting the wings of the Church that have been forced by a false dilemma into two camps—those emphasising intellectual truth at the expense of emotional experience and those rejoicing in experience at the expense of the Christian mind. Their reunification is long overdue.

Open doors of spirituality

We will explore this whole area further in Chapter 12, when we look at the spirituality of a post-Christian society—but it is important in passing to note the relevance of this theme to a post-modern faith. Divorced as it may be from any definite sense of God, post-modern culture is nonetheless wide open to spiritual experience. Spirituality is seen not as belonging to an 'other realm' beyond some great divide, but as being an aspect of human activity available to us—a muscle we may have forgotten how to use. '*Ask an Eastern guru to teach you how to pray, and he will say to you "Try this",'* a friend recently challenged me. *'Ask a Christian the same question, and she will say, "First you must believe."'* With more and more people asking the question, it is essential that we realign our answers.

Embrace technology

In modernity, technology is entirely wrapped up with the progress myth—it is one of the gods that will save us. To post-moderns, it has no such power, and is associated, rather, with play. As Mike Riddell explains,

> Postmodernists are children of technology. They embrace it enthusiastically for the enhancements it can bring to life ... and especially for its ability to increase the scope of "play". There is no longer any expectation that technology is somehow going to solve existential angst, but it may well provide better ways of escaping from it.[11]

In the shift towards postmodernity, technology has 'changed sides', from being the willing slave of metanarrative to being the enabling force of deconstruction. Digital technology is not associated with rationalism and empiricism, even though it deals for the most part with logic and is built entirely on the numbers one and zero! Post-moderns expect technology to be used to explore the experiential, the emotional and the intuitive. In practical terms, this may mean that it is as important to load the church computer with a copy of Myst as of Microsoft Office.

In the shift from progress to pessimism

Rediscover the better future

Tom Sine has said:

In a world drowning in cynicism, nihilism and polarisation, people are looking for a reason for hope. And I am convinced that the people of God have no higher calling than to offer hope to the world. The only problem is that we cannot offer what we do not possess.[12]

For Sine, the recovery of hope demands the rediscovery of God's plans for the human future—the biblical vision of a renewed cosmos and of the 'great homecoming' in which every tribe (and story) finds its place. Missiologist David Bosch makes the same plea:

We should not capitulate to pessimism and despair. All around us people are looking for new meaning in life. This is the moment where the Christian Church and the Christian mission may once again, humbly yet resolutely, present the vision of the reign of God not as pie in the sky but as an eschatological reality which casts its rays into the dismal present, illuminates it and confers meaning on it.[13]

Be ready for despair

Kurt Cobhain[14] has become an icon of post-modern youth—hating himself, despising others, ultimately taking his own life. According to reports, he had asked his record company to accept as a title for his last album *I hate Myself and I want to Die*.[15] They refused. He died. Youth suicide is growing throughout the West, as are the patterns of destructive behaviour that fall just short of it. This is where the rubber of existential angst hits the road of real young lives, where individuals grow up under such a weight of confusion, pessimism and self-loathing that, in due course, it crushes them. If there is any gospel that is going to have nothing to say to such people, it is a triumphalistic, escapist, easy-believism—the kind detractors call 'happy-clappy'. In postmodernity, Jonny Baker argues, '*pain and brokenness rather than success will connect with others*'.[16] It is not that the Christian story leaves us in our despair—but it begins by sharing the pain we feel. The irony of twenty-first century apologetics is that Christians will be called at one and the same time to proclaim hope and to empathise with despair.

On the journey from creed to community

Live it out

In prioritising abstract ideas, modernity allowed us to divorce belief from action and lifestyle—to accept propositional truth without living it out. Postmodernity, by contrast, recognises only indwelt truth. The emerging culture demands an 'embodied apologetic—a flesh-and-blood, living and breathing argument for God'.[17] Our culture is less and less interested in what the Church *believes* and more and more concerned about the way she *behaves*. To the questions postmodernism is asking, Christopher Jones has said, '*The Church's response must be to exhibit in concrete form the meaning of life lived in openness to the God of Jesus, the triune God who is Truth and Love and Goodness.*'[18] It is likely that the journey into postmodernity will produce new Christian projects and communities which are united not by a common creed, but by a common lifestyle. The appeal of these communities to the wider culture will not so much be 'join us if you believe these things' as 'join us if you want to live this way'. Once again, this is a reversal of polarity, from churches in which dogma is essential and lifestyle optional, to churches built on lifestyle leaving dogma to personal choice.

Build community

According to Jimmy Long, 'Christians in the emerging post-modern era are beginning to see that they need to re-emphasise relational community'.[19] Long quotes Gareth

Icenogle as saying, 'Jesus' mission was to demonstrate the nearness of God to alienated humanity. To do this he formed small group communities.'[20] Icenogle makes the claim that 'tribalism, or community, is much more closely aligned than the autonomous self to God's intention'.[21] The post-modern generation, then, will look for more than off-the-shelf truth, more even than truth embodied in an individual life. They will look for truth indwelt within a community or tribe. Like anthropologists breaking into the depths of the Amazon rainforest, they will ask themselves, 'What makes this tribe tick? What are the norms of this community?' No amount of persuasive preaching will mend the damage if the lived-out answers to these questions are off-putting. The post-modern generation are looking for authenticity, reality, transparency and openness. To the extent that postmodernity is saying, 'Don't talk to me about what you believe—show me how you live,' it is entirely biblical—more so, at times, than the Church it so savagely critiques.

Believe in friendship

Long makes the observation that the post-modern genera-tion are turning more and more to their friends as a new family. 'Why is it,' he asks, 'that in the mid-1990s the most popular and copied TV programme is *Friends*? In the 1950s we were immersed in family TV shows . . . today the themes of many shows centre around friends, not family.'[22] Mike Riddell supports this view, writing that:

> In the absence of transcendent values or meanings, partici-pants in the new culture are finding significance in friendship. . . Not just in sexual or romantic couplings, but in a lively sense of community expressed among groups of friends. It is a new social tribalism among those who recognise in others something of their own experience.[23]

It is likely that these new dynamics of community flowing along the lines of friendship will become the natural seams of the emerging culture, so much so that church structures and plans which cut across them will be hotly challenged. The Church has for many years understood the need to grow with, rather than against, the natural currents of family; now she must learn to respect, too, the lines of friendship. Small-group communities which build on the strengths of friendship will have a lasting quality far in excess of larger structures which ignore them.

In the conflict of commitment vs choice and change

Embrace process and journey

If there is any one aspect of Christian practice that is roundly challenged by postmodernity, it is a turnstile understanding of conversion—the view that a single decision, made in a moment, is enough to secure lifelong commitment. The huge success of the Alpha course, which presses for commitment but does so in the context of process and journey, is indicative of this change. In postmodernity, the journey of faith is not a one-off crossroads at which both destiny and destination are sealed, but a series of junctions and forks in the road—at each of which choices must be made. Discipleship, in this context, is never about a short-term sales experience but is always about a long-term, ongoing relationship.

Revalidate faith experience

It follows that Christian experience, on this journey, requires frequent revalidation. No assumption can be made that a decision of last month or last year will still hold good next week. The new-found emphasis among young people on the experiential dimension of faith is a symptom of this need for revalidation, as is the revival in a sacramental view of the Eucharist—in which the Christian story is rehearsed, and the response of repentance relived, week by week. In one, post-modern young people want to check that God is still moving, in the other they check that they are still moved. Repeated spiritual experiences confirm that God is still in business, and that the magnetic power of the Christian story is still strong.

Celebrate diversity

Lack of choice is an abiding characteristic of modernity, offering one truth, one standard, one-size-fits-all. Post-modernity, by contrast, is extreme in its desire for choice. The Church, says Nick Mercer, is in an ideal position to meet this change.

> In a post-modern society where choice is of the essence of life, the Church is in a strong position, with 57 varieties to suit most tastes and temperaments, all with one central, Christological and Trinitarian message. If only we could celebrate that diversity and love one another.[24]

The Church's calling '*is not to monolithic unity but to reconciled diversity*'.[25] To borrow a phrase from D. Martin Fields, a Church expressing the true richness of Christian diversity will be '*not a melting pot but a salad bowl*'.[26]

Emphasis homecoming

Post-moderns are not looking for a set of propositions to assent to, they are looking for a place to live. If Christianity is to work for them, it must become their home—the place of security from which the world is explored and understood. They will not bring only their 'souls' or brains into the household, but the whole of their lives—the good, the bad and the ugly. An invitation to this generation that is founded on anything other than unconditional love will fall on deaf ears.

This is by no means a comprehensive strategy for engaging the post-modern generations. But it is a series of starting points—doorways into a re-imagined Church. Like many others, I have struggled to come to terms with some of the changes implied here. There are many issues in which conclusions remain unclear, but I do sense a growing momentum in the Church's desire to truly engage the emerging culture. I share with Ian Cundy, Bishop of Lewes, both the sense of postmodernity as a mixed blessing and the urgency of the task of engagement:

> It is not surprising therefore that our view of the post-modern is mixed. Caution and excitement, criticism and enthusiasm are all present in some measure. But one thing remains our common concern. The task of understanding our context, however difficult, cannot be avoided if we are to be faithful to our mission. It is in and to this context that the gospel is addressed.[27]

Notes

1 Graham Cray, quoted in David Hillborn, *Picking Up the Pieces* (Hodder and Stoughton: London, 1997), p. 5.
2 Kevin Ford, *Jesus for a New Generation* (Hodder and Stoughton: London, 1996), p. 130.
3 For a review of Hook, see http://ecreations.com/movies/reviews/h/hook.shtml
4 Nigel Wright in Graham Cray et al, *The Post-Evangelical Debate* (Triangle: London, 1997), p. 99.
5 Graham Cray in Cray et al, *op. cit.*, pp. 2, 15.

6 J. Richard Middleton and Brian J. Walsh, *op. cit.*, p. 107.

7 *Ibid.*, p. 189.

8 Nick Mercer in Cray et al, *op. cit.*, p. 44.

9 Walter James and Brian Russel, 'How has postmodernism changed education?', *Tomorrow is Another Country* (Board of Education of the General Synod of the Church of England: London, 1996), p. 27.

10 Kevin Ford, *op. cit.*, p. 130.

11 Mike Riddell, *Threshold of the Future: Reforming the Church in the Post-Christian West* (SPCK: London, 1998), p. 111.

12 Tom Sine, *Cease Fire: Searching for Sanity in America's Culture Wars* (Eerdmans: Grand Rapids, Mi., 1995), p. 224.

13 David Bosch, *Transforming Mission* (Orbis Books: New York, 1993), p. 361.

14 For background to Cobhain's career, see http://www.escape. ca/~grsd/

15 Mike Riddell, *op. cit.*, p. 108.

16 Jonny Baker leads the Grace service in Ealing, London. Private conversation.

17 Kevin Ford, *op. cit.*, p. 179.

18 Christopher Jones, in *Tomorrow is Another Country*, p. 23.

19 Jimmy Long, *Generating Hope* (IVP: Downers Grove, Ill., 1997), p. 100.

20 Gareth Icenogle, *Biblical Foundations for Small Group Ministry* (IVP: Downers Grove, Ill., 1994), p. 118, quoted in Jimmy Long, *op. cit.*, p. 90.

21 Jimmy Long, *op. cit.*, p. 84.

22 Jimmy Long, *op. cit.*, p. 50.

23 Mike Riddell, *op. cit.*, p. 110.

24 Nick Mercer in Cray et al, *op. cit.*, p. 60.

25 Christopher Jones, *op. cit.*

26 D. Martin Fields, *op. cit.*

27 Ian Cundy, 'Catching the (last) Post', in *Tomorrow is Another Country*, p. 90.

10

THE POWER OF GLOBFRAG
The Post-imperial World Order

Mickey is universal. He's just as popular in Moscow and Leningrad—these places where he's never been. There's all these rip-offs in copyright terms all over the world. He's on every T-shirt in the world—I saw him in the wilds of New Guinea five years ago.

Roy E. Disney, *Empire Magazine*, 1989[1]

Sadly, what is happening around us today, this horror, this chaos on our soil, in the heart of Europe, at the beginning of the twenty-first century, this destruction, this killing, this hatred—this, alas, is no dream but a living nightmare.

Boro Todorovic, UTEL TV, Belgrade, 1991[2]

The empires strikes out

For generations the Bosnian city of Mostar[3]—economic, industrial and cultural centre of the province of Herzogovina—was the 'Jewel of the South', a popular and renowned tourist destination. 'On the banks of the playful Neretva', intones a brochure from the days of Tito, 'lies a town of unequalled beauty—a harmonious link between oriental and Western architecture . . . Nature divided this town with water, man linked it with bridges.' A remarkable gateway between East and West, where ancient empires met and Christian and Muslim civilisations merged, Mostar's centrepiece was the ancient *Stari Most* (Old Bridge), a high-arched, graceful stone structure recognised as one of the architectural treasures of the Balkans. Centuries ago, it was the *Mostari*, the bridge-keepers who patrolled this and other crossings of the steep and winding Neretva Valley, who gave this city its name. But the Stari Most was more than a stone span stretched across a river valley: it was a bridge across cultures, a visible symbol of a city in which people groups with very different histories worked together to a common future.

Today the Stari Most, like much of Mostar, is reduced to dust and rubble. April 1992 marked the beginning of thirty-two months of shelling, sniper-fire and house-to-house fighting that left Mostar as a city with its heart torn out. Death, injury, bereavement, hunger, displacement, anger and destruction became the bitter daily fare of those who stayed. Thousands more left; many will never return. The evil that convulsed the body of the former Yugoslavia like a territorial fit found its epi-centre in Bosnia—and Mostar, the jewel that once was, was shaken to its core. This was not a war waged against a powerful invader—it was a war of neighbour against neighbour, a virulent, stupefying violence that turned ordinary men and women into killers and the streets of the city into an apocalyptic nightmare. It will take years, generations even, for Mostar to recover.

Mostar is one city among many in the former Yugoslavia, one battle-zone among many the world over. Its shelled-out ruins stand as a symbol of one of the most powerful and dangerous currents of the closing years of the twentieth century. The break-up of empires; the redrawing of borders;

the sudden proliferation, across the planet, of ethnic and territorial conflict—these are the symptoms of a process so powerful that it leaves hardly a corner of the earth untouched: the unfolding of a post-imperial world order. This has been a decade in which bridges have been both built and destroyed.

In its simplest form, post-imperialism has meant that the huge colonial empires that dominated the world at the birth of the twentieth Century have broken up in time for its demise. The film *Titanic*, with its strong sub-theme of class differentiation, is a timely reminder to contemporary generations of just how strong the imperial spirit was, even as recently as 1912. The Great War was perhaps the last stand of colonial assumptions, and the decades which followed it saw the slow unravelling of imperial powers—a process which continues to this day. At one end of the transaction the former colonies have sought independence and self-rule, while at the other their former colonial powers are coming to terms with the imperial legacy as they evolve into multi-cultural, multi-ethnic societies.

Even before the dust had settled on the collapse of the once-mighty colonialism, the final decade of the century brought the astounding news of the end both of Soviet communism and of the South African system of apartheid. If there was any doubt that the monolithic empires were breaking up, it was swept away in 1989 when the falling masonry of the Berlin Wall[4] signalled the crumbling of the political system it had so darkly symbolised. The Eastern bloc disintegrated and the hundreds of ethno-linguistic groups under its gaze began to rediscover self-identity and the hunger for self-rule. '*From Azerbaijan to the Baltic*,' writes Marcus Tanner, '*nations long buried under the rubble of empire have risen to claim a place in the sun.*'[5] Who could have believed that the generation that witnessed these historic changes would also see the inauguration of President Nelson Mandela, perhaps the world's most potent symbol of the end of the imperial age.

Not one force but two

If imperialism was characterised by the subjugation of small nations and people-groups into monolithic empires—whether colonial or communist—and by the forced abandonment of cultural identity, the post-imperial age will be marked by the self-identification of an ever more complex kaleidoscope of ethnic and social groups. The key to understanding this process is the recognition that its momentum is derived not from one force but from two. The twin but opposing forces of *globalisation* and *fragmentation*—the one drawing the world together, the other tearing it apart—form the double-act at the heart of a whole range of contemporary conflicts. This is the power of globfrag, the most significant force at work in contemporary global politics. Philosopher Michael Ignatieff[6] dramatically captures the counteraction of these forces:

> The more evident our common needs as a species become, the more brutal becomes the human insistence on the claims of difference. The centripetal forces of need, labour and science which are pulling us together as a species are counter-balanced by centrifugal forces, the claims of tribe, race, class, section, region and nation, pulling us apart.[7]

The post-imperialism of the coming decades will be the child of these mis-matched parents. This is the reality described by Benjamin R. Barber as 'Jihad vs McWorld'. 'McDonald's in Moscow and Coke in China will do more to create a global culture than military colonisation ever could,'[8] he writes. But at the same time, 'There were more than thirty wars in progress last year, most of them ethnic, racial, tribal or religious in character, and the list of unsafe regions doesn't seem to be getting any shorter. Some new world order!'[9]

Somewhere in the mysterious interplay of globalisation and fragmentation, in the cross-currents of human identity and aspiration, lies the dynamic tension that will characterise not only nations but neighbourhoods in the early twenty-first century. This is a tension that surfaces not only in the planet's ethnic hot-spots, but also on the streets of cities the world over, as young people ask 'Who am I?' The youth of Beirut holding high a Kalashnikov and wearing chest-bands of bullets may be a symbol of the struggle for identity—but so is the child of Moss Side and the Bronx, armed only with a spray can, out to make a mark on the world.

Definitions

The world of Generation X and beyond will be post-imperial in the sense that:

1. The old global context built on the assumptions of empires, colonies and mono-cultural rule will have finally given way.
2. In its place, a new world order will emerge founded on the competitive multiplicity of the planetary marketplace.
3. The twin forces by which this new order is shaped will be those of *globalisation* and *fragmentation*.
4. The tension of these forces will be felt not only among nations but within nations, as the nation-state itself is shaken by cultural fragmentation.

The purpose of this chapter will be to explore the broad contours of this post-imperial world and the implications of globfrag. For the Western Church, these implications will surface in two distinct areas:

1. In its understanding of mission—the global dynamic of the Church's identity and task. If mission in the past has carried with it imperial values, what values will carry mission into the future?
2. In its engagement with the generations impacted 'at home' by the power of globfrag—generations swept up in globalisation, torn apart by fragmentation and struggling for identity.

Not surprisingly, there is a significant overlap between the historical progress of post-imperialism and the philosophical development of postmodernism, which speaks of 'hearing all the stories' and 'bringing the margins into the centre'. What the philosophy asks us *in theory* to consider, world history is asking us *in practice* to embrace. To some extent this overlap explains the remarkable speed at which post-modern theory has gripped the hearts and minds of our culture—because it speaks into a context already taken up with the questions it addresses. The pragmatic, hands-on, people-centred, real-world questions of globfrag will put arms and legs on the Church's response to its post-modern context. Our exploration of these themes will first examine the nature and interplay of globalisation and fragmentation, before going on to consider their implications.

You and your mall corner

Globalisation is a real and powerful force. It has shaped the world in the closing years of the twentieth century and it will go on doing so in the early decades of the twenty-first.

At the heart of globalisation lie the new possibilities of commerce, travel and communication opened up by the technologies of our time. Commerce delivers more products than ever on a global scale, travel carries individuals to diverse and far-flung destinations and communication brings the cultures of the world onto screens, speakers and telephone receivers in the intimacy of our own homes. The fuel that has enabled us to exploit these possibilities at such an alarming speed is the fuel of consumerism—the drive to deliver more goods to more people in more places than ever before.

The growth of the literal *McWorld*[10] is a measure of this. In 1966 McDonald's operated fast-food outlets in one nation—the USA. By 1976 they were represented in 21 countries, and by 1986 in 45. By the late 1990s the chain included 18,000 restaurants in 94 countries on 5 continents—a growth rate to rival that of any religion the world has ever known. 'I am open to any course that helps McDonald dominate every market,' says Chairman of the Board, Michael Quinlan.[11] Add to McWorld the names of Coke, MTV, Disney, Dreamworks, Michael Jordan, Madonna, Microsoft, Nintendo and the hundreds like them, and the scale of global culture begins to become clear. Never before have the diverse cultures of the world been exposed to so many common products. The rising generations of the coming decades will reap the fruit of a world remoulded by these forces—recognising no community but the market and no authority but the customer who pays—as they deliver unprecedented levels of globalism in the twenty-first century.

The children of the 21st century will inherit a world in many ways beguiling. For everyone but the poorest, it beckons as a magical empire of Mammon, a madcap consumer's paradise of immediate gratification and express delivery, of hot images and cool gadgets, of designer jeans and designer genes.[12]

But this is not the only story. 'Beneath the surface all is not well . . . the modern economy masks a disfigured planet.'[13] While much is positive in the rise of globalism, not least the breaking-down of barriers, there is also much to be wary of.

Are you being serfed?

Tom Sine is in no doubt of the role of commercial interests in the drive towards a global culture, nor of the challenge that this represents for the Christian faith community:

> Economic globalisation is being advanced by powerful financiers, influential CEOs of trans-national corporations and international political brokers. None of us were given an opportunity to vote whether we or our respective countries wanted to be part of a one world economic order . . . It's like going to sleep in your bed in your own home and waking up jammed into a gigantic global rocket ship with 6 billion others all hurtling through space at fantastic speeds with absolutely no notion of the destination.[14]

Sine characterises God's plan for the human future as a different kind of globalism, the 'mustard seed' variety that has:

> More to do with making a difference than with making a dollar . . . more to do with creating a new reconciled global community of justice and celebration than with the production of a new global community of consumption . . . more to do with coming home to Jerusalem than Babylon.[15]

He poses the question that must be at the heart of the Christian Church's agenda in the years that lie ahead—which will prove stronger, mustard seed or McWorld?

The coca-colonisation of youth

As targets in an increasing proportion of planet-wide marketing, young people are at the epi-centre of this globalisation storm. One of the most telling side-effects of trans-national consumerism is that it gives young people more commonality with their global peers than with the former generations of their own home cultures. Colin Morris writes:

> Since all cultures have to locate themselves in time and space, oral societies had a sense of continuity over time, but were spatially discontinuous. Things were reasonably harmonious between generations within the same society, but there were vast differences and often conflicts with other societies a hundred miles or so apart. Time bound oral societies together, space separated them. When oral cultures gave place first to print and then to the electronic media ... the relationship between time and space was reversed. ... It was space which became continuous because the airwaves could annihilate distance.[16]

This is the origin of the generation gap, described by communications theorist James W. Carey in 1969 as the process by which 'The axis of diversity shifts from a spatial ... to a temporal or generational dimension'.[17] While the opening of this gap was first seen in the 1960s, the transitional generations of more recent decades are the first to be fully formed in its context—young people shaped more than ever in history by an awareness of the planetary scale of their own generation:

Young people around the world are not suddenly the members of one homogenous people group—but they operate more and more in one market-place. More and more they seek points of reference among their generational peers rather than their geographical elders. More and more they are shaped by the same global forces, many of them commercial, despite the great distances that separate them. For some the need to belong, the longing for roots and tribe, has been transferred entirely to generational peers . . . . they no longer want to belong to anyone but each other.[18]

This radical shift represents a huge challenge to the Christian faith community, which for the most part still assumes time to be continuous and space discontinuous. No indigenous church can assume any longer that the passing of the faith to the new generation will be an easy, natural process. Nor can any one culture assume that its chosen 'flavour of faith' will be attractive to its young. Communicating faith across the generational divide is fast becoming as significant a cross-cultural challenge as communicating across oceans once was.

Balkanisation bites back

If evidence for the progress of globalisation is overwhelming, so is that for the pain of fragmentation, and the rising generations of young people and children are, once again, caught in the cross-fire.

The dropping of the atom bomb on Hiroshima in 1945 sent a chilling message to an entire generation, and led to the superpower deadlock that became known as the Cold War. Somehow this deadlock averted global war. But at the same time, small-scale wars using conventional weapons reached epidemic proportions, with over 200 wars world-wide since 1945.

> Globalisation has kept a kind of peace, but fragmentation has let loose a different kind of war.[19]

This is the greatest irony of the late twentieth century, that an era of peace has also been an era of war. There are no signs that this violent fragmentation—nations literally tearing themselves apart—is abating, and the world enters its third millennium with an unprecedented number and range of actual and potential conflicts. 'The Leviathan seems to have seized the global village and taken its inhabitants hostage,' writes Felix 'Machi Njoku of the situation facing Africa. 'Henceforth, the law of the jungle reigns supreme and only the strong can escape from its clutches.'[20]

Even contained at current levels, the degree of violence attributed around the world to ethnic break-up is sufficient to render fragmentation one of the primary driving forces of the new century.

Patchwork populations

Within nations, not least in the vast sprawl of multi-cultural cities, the same fault-lines are being projected from the global to the local scale. The world's mega-cites are growing as patchwork quilts of diverse and varied cultures. In many ways a city is a microcosm of the planet, playing out on its own scale the warring forces of globfrag. Globalisation is present in the melting-pot effect, as diverse ethnic groups living in close proximity lose some of their distinctives. But fragmentation is also present as those same groups, lost in the urban vastness, struggle with issues of identity. It is no longer possible to identify a people group primarily in terms of their geographical location. Patrick Johnstone's *Operation World*[21] defines a 'people group' as 'a significantly large sociological grouping of individuals who perceive themselves to have a common affinity'.[22]

Johnstone recognises three types of group: *ethno-linguistic*—defined primarily by language and ethnicity; *sociological*—defined by a long-term relation to the wider society such as a traditional occupation or class, and *incidental*—defined by temporary or circumstantial factors, such as high-rise dwellers, drug users or commuters. Explaining the counting of such groups, Johnstone says, 'the Tamil are counted 23 times in the global totals because Tamil communities exist in at least 23 countries, likewise the Kurds 20 times, the Sininke of West Africa 6 times.'[23] Nations, cities and neighbourhoods may contain dozens of sub-cultural groups, each participating in the unity of civic life, but each retaining in some measure its own identity. The coming century will present us with an over-abundance of threatened peoples retreating into old and new tribal shells, in societies shattered like a broken mirror into thousands of pieces. An approach that assumes one dominant cultural identity for a given city or region will run counter to the whole flow of history, and the Christian Church will face the challenges of cross-cultural mission as much 'on home turf' as abroad. This is the case already in significant sectors of inner-city populations—but as globalisation and fragmentation increase in power, and play out their deadly game, it will become the case for every church, in every sector.

Notes

1 Roy E. Disney interviewed in *Empire Magazine*, December 1989, quoted in Alan MacDonald, *Films in Close-Up* (IVP, 1991).
2 Statement made by the Belgrade actor Boro Todorovic to the TV Station UTEL, 2 November 1991, quoted in Misha Glenny, *The Fall of Yugoslavia* (Penguin, London, 1992), preface.

3   For information on Mostar, see http://encarta.msn.com/
    index/conciseindex/6E/06ECC000.htm
4   For a history of the Berlin Wall in words, pictures and music,
    see http://members.aol.com/johball/berlinwl.htm
5   Marcus Tanner, 'Will the Kurds Ever Be a Nation?', *The Inde-
    pendent*, London, 15 January 1999.
6   For Ignatieff articles, see http://www.oneworld.org/index_oc/
    issue397/ignatieff.htm
7   Michael Ignatieff, *The Needs of Strangers* (Chatto and Windus:
    London, 1984), p. 130.
8   Benjamin R. Barber, 'Jihad vs McWorld', in *The Atlantic
    Monthly*, Vol. 269, No. 3, March 1992, p. 58.
9   *Ibid.*, p. 60.
10 http://www.mcdonalds.com
11 Quoted in Tom Sine, *Mustard Seed versus McWorld* (Monarch:
    Crowborough, 1999).
12 Eugene Linden, 'What Have We Wrought?', in *Time Maga-
    zine*, November 1997.
13 *Ibid.*
14 Tom Sine, *op. cit.*
15 *Ibid.*
16 Colin Morris, *God in a Box* (Hodder and Stoughton: London,
    1984).
17 Quoted in Alvin Toffler, *Future Shock* (Pan Books: New York,
    1970).
18 Gerard Kelly and Lowell Sheppard, *Their Future our Passion*
    (Youth for Christ International: Singapore, 1996).
19 *Ibid.*
20 Felix 'Machi Njoku, 'Watch Out: Globalisation is Re-drawing
    Africa's Borders', Panafrican News Agency, Internet article,
    27 January 1998. http://www.africanews.org/PANA/news/
    19980127/feat1.html
21 http://www.gmi.org/products/owdf.htm
22 Patrick Johnstone, *Operation World* (OM Publishing: Carlisle,
    1993).
23 *Ibid.*

11

PICKING UP THE PIECES
Living in the Post-imperial World

*No country can build an unbreachable wall around itself. The
image of vast armies of wretched poor, surging around the globe
and clamouring at the borders of the more fortunate nations, may
finally awaken the world to the kind of future that today's leaders may be foisting on the next generation*

Eugene Linden[1]

It takes a broken generation to reach a broken world

Barrie Taylor[2]

If these two forces of globalisation and fragmentation are
set to shape not only the 'world order' of international relations but also the domestic order of Western, urban culture,
what challenges do they present to the Church's response to
the transitional generations? What can we expect the impact
of globfrag to be?

1. The cry of unheard voices

The challenge to engage at a deep level with an increasingly
multi-cultural society, both at home and abroad, brings
with it the challenge to renounce once and for all the limited

and limiting paradigms of a Euro-centric theology. Two examples of this process at work serve to illustrate not only the necessity but also the cost of such a renunciation—and the fruitfulness it can bring.

Robert Beckford is a black Pentecostal theologian who has extensively researched Christian thought and practice in the UK's multi-cultural context. Engagement with such a context requires us, he says, to change the way we 'do' theology. 'The white academic establishment's monopoly in defining, doing and validating theology in Britain,' he says, 'renders Black Christianity and its theologies invisible.'[3] It is not that theology necessarily bars participation on the basis of skin-colour, but that it makes cultural assumptions which, by default, exclude ethnic diversity. Beckford continues:

> Black Christian theological thought is difficult to express using traditional Western categories because, in most white-led denominations, professional theologians, primarily white, male and elitist, "do theology" on behalf of their churches. In the main they use methods, concepts and resources which have emerged from European history, thought and experience.[4]

Writing from a North-American perspective, commentator H. P. Spees sees much the same situation in place.

> To see ethnocentrism in the church, one need look no further than the Christian bookstore, Sunday School material and the offerings of seminars in the United States. Within the Evangelical Christian community, alternatives other than those shaped by the values of the white dominant culture are by far the exception rather than the rule.[5]

Robert Beckford's responses include evaluating Dread culture, exploring black images of Jesus and using the lyrics of Bob Marley as a source for theological reflection[6]—all of which produce new and fresh insights into key aspects of the Christian faith. The post-imperial world will demand not only that we embrace the work of such theologians as Robert Beckford, but that we extend and encourage the spread of a similar theological process into other ethnic and cultural groups.

A more widely-known example of post-imperialism at work in the Church is that of Japanese theologian Kosuke Koyami. A gifted and able scholar, Koyami became a missionary to Thailand, where:

> He decided that he must subordinate great theological thoughts, like those of Thomas Aquinas and Karl Barth, to the needs of the farmers. He gave priority to the farmers over Aquinas and Barth because he was preaching in Thailand, not in Italy or Switzerland.[7]

Koyami's willingness to uproot theology from its cultural setting and reroot it in a local community produced a rich vein of insight and achievement—better theology, in effect, than that which he might have attained had he kept within safe boundaries. An example of the fruitfulness of this expressly non-Western approach was his book *Three Mile an Hour God.*

> God walks 'slowly' because he is love . . . Love has its speed. It is an inner speed. It is a spiritual speed. It is a different kind of speed from the technological speed to which we are accustomed . . . It goes on in the depth of our life, whether we notice or not, whether we are currently hit by storm or not, at three miles an hour. It is the speed we walk and therefore it is the speed the love of God walks.[8]

Both Koyami and Beckford illustrate how much Western thinking has to gain from the renunciation of its white, male, European exclusivity. This is not a preoccupation only for theologians—it must be allowed to spill over into the everyday world of church culture. How much of the cultural exclusivity of our faith is invested not in our belief structures but in seemingly innocent, ground-level practice—the music we listen to and use, the language we adopt, the clothes we wear, the images and illustrations with which we choose to explain our faith? These different factors add up to a corporate body language, sending out messages whether we know it or not. As does the visible mix and make-up of our leadership and staff—those we allow to exercise public authority.

> Do we . . . suffer from the blindness of mono-cultural leadership? . . . We must hire, partner with, pray with, shape our organisation[s] to make room for, support, serve, raise money for existing leaders from disenfranchised cultures, and include them in whatever way possible at the highest levels of our organisation[s].[9]

More and more the twin forces of globalisation and fragmentation are throwing a spotlight onto the cultural bias in our churches, and giving a voice to those long silenced. To the extent that post-imperialism leads us to listen to the powerless, to give voice to the marginalised, to see through the eyes of the poor, it is a thoroughly biblical process. If the twenty-first century demands of us that we embrace cultural diversity and renounce the power-structures that prosperity and good fortune have enabled us to build, then it is doing no less than calling us back to the foundations of our faith.

2. Advertainment and alienation

If the forces of globalisation and fragmentation produce anything 'on the street' it is a crisis of identity. Young people cut off from the fading appeal of their tribal roots, but unable to find their place in the new global village, come to live in an emotional and cultural no-man's-land best captured in the term alienation. The 1985 *Faith in the City* report, working at the extreme end of economic deprivation, dramatically described the lives of such young people.

> The overall impression is clear. It is that there are sizeable groups of young people who are trapped in Urban Priority Areas, who only gain attention when they become a threat, who are denied equality of life chances, and with whom the churches have little or no contact. It is difficult to exaggerate how alienated these people are: from adult ideas of how young people should behave; from their peers of different social classes; from agencies they think of as acting on adults' behalf and not in the interests of young people, e.g. from the police; from school; and from the church.[10]

The irony of the new 'global youth club' is that the one thing young people most share the world over is this sense of lostness. If alienation is its bitter fruit, then advertainment is the power that drives it. The glittering appeal of global culture draws the young away from any sense of tribal or family rootedness, but offers nothing of substance in its place. Aimed at stimulating the needs of the marketplace, at locating dissatisfaction and driving it home, advertainment is, by definition, designed to disappoint— MTVessels make the most noise.

Psychologist Oliver James is in no doubt of the link of such alienation both to social fragmentation and to the immense power of the consumer machine. 'The collapse of marriage and of the close social networks that characterised our ancestors is a major cause of ... depression, aggression, compulsions.'[11] Looking at the lives of those (often men) in whom such alienation is expressed in violent behaviour, he adds, 'They contrast the consumer goods, the permissive lifestyle and the self-focussed opportunism of the media role models offered on film and television with the reality of their own lives.'[12]

If the Christian Church is unable to confront this lostness in the new generations—if it fails to confront the power of advertainment and the wild aspirations it brings, and to deal with the core issues of identity, status, attachment and community—then it will lose its foothold in the cultures of the twenty-first century. The challenge is to provide both roots and wings—to bring young people into a sense of connectedness with the past that doesn't rob them of their vision for the future. Tony Campolo[13] explains this 'roots and wings' philosophy in the context in which it is most easily applied—the family:

> Roots. The parent must communicate to the child a sense of stability, of security; a sense of belonging so that who I am is firmly established and what our family stands for is firmly defined. The family must also provide wings. That is, it must create in children a sense of imagination ... To imagine what they could be ... what the future might be ... To dream dreams—to help a child believe in herself.[14]

In some cases this requires the validation of a person's known roots, affirming the strength and dignity of the tribe and history from which they come even when this falls outside of the Church's dominant norms. In others, it requires the provision of a new history—a foster-tribe able to give identity to those so cut off from their past that no personal history remains. In both cases, and all between, it requires the recognition, in a world cut loose of its moorings, that roots and relationships matter, that the need for love is the one need that our culture most stimulates and least meets. Catching the cry of those lost in the headlong rush to the global mall, Mike Riddell writes,

> The trendy word for being lost is alienation . . . It is an ache in the deepest part of you, a longing which nothing in the world ever quite touches . . . the sense of being lost comes like a fragment of a song . . . Finding the way is all about coming home.[15]

3. New tribes born

Oliver James goes on to explore the relationship of cultural alienation to gang culture, in which those under pressure 'create alternative sub-cultures in which their attributes— impulsiveness, aggression, nothing to lose—are valuable . . . In the wider society's terms they may be losers but in their subculture, they can be on top of the world.'[16] Walsh and Middleton write that:

> The escalation of fascist ideology among teens in Europe and the multiplication of inner-city gangs in North America, often with a narrowly conceived ethnic identity, is further evidence of the desperate need to belong to a group and inhabit a meaningful story, even a narrow and violent one, so long as it gives identity and purpose.[17]

Gang culture is the urban expression of the same destructive forces which, on a global scale, produce ethnic and genocidal conflicts.

Ironically, gang culture has itself become a favoured brand-image of the global youth club, with music and fashions forged in the street-battles of Chicago and LA transformed into cultural product for export to the world. In a watered-down form, gang culture becomes the new tribalism of youth, with millions of young people the world over seeking identity in coded signs of commonality. New tribes spring up with unprecedented speed as sub-cultures give birth to sub-sub-cultures; groups within groups gathering around ever more complex and specific distinctions—and often replicated in mirror-image groups thousands of miles and several continents away. The drive among the young to seek identity and status in the external signs of tribalism is probably one of the strongest and deepest currents in our present situation. The evident truth that 'Culture has meaning precisely because it differs from other cultures'[18] pushes young people not only to choose an identity, but to express it in divisive or hostile terms. Even if the powerful forces of globalisation and fragmentation were to stabilise tomorrow, millions of young people would still be dealing, for years to come, with the effects of gang culture.

4. Old tribes born again

9 August 1998 was officially designated 'Indigenous People's Day', and the United Nations has declared a 'Decade of Indigenous Peoples'. While urban gangs carve out new tribes for themselves, there are old tribes—some as old as human civilisation itself—restating their claim to self-rule. 'The cause of the planet's myriad indigenous populations is gaining ground,' writes Rupert Cornwell. 'In the last 20 years, the total number of tribal peoples has risen, Survival International (the largest campaigning group for indigenous peoples) estimates, from 200m to 300m.'[19]

At the heart of the struggle of indigenous peoples are the questions of land and culture. In cases such as those of

Australian and North American native peoples, the conflict is over land taken from them in the past. In cases such as those of the Amazon rainforests or of Irian Jaya, the Indonesian half of New Guinea, it is land being taken even now. Usually at the centre of such a conflict there is a question of profit—most often from mining and forestry rights—but there are other, less measurable factors: the submerging of a culture; the refusal to acknowledge traditional views of nature, land and ownership; the loss of a way of life.

> And so it goes the world over. You can see it in the clusters of dispossessed, drink-ravaged aborigines at encampments in the dried out watercourse of the Todd River at Alice Springs. You see it in the mosquito-ridden swamps of north-west Siberia where the local Khanty and Mansi hunters and herders lament a way of life submerged beneath the foul lakes of crude oil spewed forth by the Soviet-era rigs. The Khanty do not want the full proceeds of what is among the richest oilfields on earth . . . merely their land as they once knew it.[20]

There can be no doubt that the crisis of identity of the world's indigenous peoples, and the echoes of guilt among those who have wronged them, will continue well into the twenty-first century. The rediscovery of the rights of such peoples; the questioning of the imperial and industrial assumptions that sought to blot them out; the re-evaluation of the contributions of 'native peoples' to human art and civilisation—these will be significant strands in the twenty-first century world view, and a shaping influence on its young generations.

5. Lazarus and Dives—a game of two halves

Not only does advertainment accentuate and fuel divisions within cultures—it is increasingly seeping across international borders to accent the growing gap between rich and poor, empowered and powerless, propertied and dispossessed. *Time Magazine*, in October 1995, published new figures which estimated the per capita wealth of the world's nations taking account not only of hard cash but of human resources, produced assets and natural capital. On this basis, the top five nations of the world each held over $500,000 (US dollars) per person, led by Australia at $835,000—while the bottom eleven all held less than $3,000 per person, with Ethiopia the lowest at $1,400. If these figures are accurate, the average Australian is 600 times richer than the average Ethiopian: a rich-poor divide on the scale of the Grand Canyon.

> The world has 358 billionaires, and their combined assets exceed the total annual income of nearly half the global population. . . . If it continues, the rich-poor divide—at individual and country level—will produce a world 'gargantuan' in its excesses and grotesque in its economic inequalities .[21]

This growing gap between the haves and the have-nots is about more than paper wealth—for the world's children it is a matter of life and death. According to a 1993 World Bank report on global healthcare:

> In the Irish Republic only 10 children per 1,000 live births dies before the age of five . . . In South America the average equivalent figure is 54, in East Asia 57, in South Asia 131 and in sub-Saharan Africa 183. In some African countries almost one third of all children die before they are five.[22]

The difference is not always about physical distance—one of the features of globalisation and fragmentation is that the geographical gap between rich and poor is often less pronounced than the economic gap seems to imply. 'A child born in 1991 in Romania, or even in Turkey, on the borders of the European Union is five times more likely to die in the first year of life than a child born in Switzerland' says the same World Bank report.[23]

As the consumer markets of the developed world expand and accelerate, the gap between the haves and the have-nots is growing, with little real prospect of significant change. As Matthew Connelly and Paul Kennedy have written:

> We are heading into the twenty-first century in a world consisting for the most part of a relatively small number of rich, satiated, demographically stagnant societies and a large number of poverty-stricken, resource-depleted nations whose populations are doubling every twenty-five years or less. The demographic imbalances are exacerbated by grotesque disparities of wealth between rich and poor countries.[24]

It is a bitter irony of this two-speed race that the consumer lifestyle, with its rapid-fire images of success, prosperity and the satisfied life, is more widely broadcast than ever. Not only are millions denied a place at the feast, but they are reminded, day in day out, of just what they are missing. In the 1997 crisis in Albania, as thousands crowded onto small boats to cross the narrow gap of sea to Italy, observers commented that for months many had been watching the commercial excess of Italian TV. When there was no bread in the shops of Albania, its people were watching adverts in which cat food was served on silver trays.[25]

Whether through such close media links, or through the explosive growth of the world's mega-cities, the poor are increasingly shown, close up, the lifestyles of the rich. In world-class cities, the haves and the have-nots share the same streets, living in daily proximity but rarely having any meaningful contact. Like Lazarus and Dives: close neighbours with entirely different lives.

For the Church, the challenge is to choose which neighbour—Lazarus or Dives—we most identify with. When Mahatma Ghandi travelled to Buckingham Palace to meet King George V, he did so wearing only his habitual loin-cloth. Asked afterwards if he had thus felt at a disadvantage, he replied cheerfully, 'Oh no, His Majesty was wearing enough for both of us.'[26] We would do well to consider which of these two leaders our own church most resembles—the king decked out in enough finery for two or the diminutive figure wearing only a simple cloth.

6. The age of the unclear family

Running in parallel with the forces of cultural fragmentation, Western culture is living through a significant decline in the status of the family. If the twentieth century has been, perhaps unwisely, the era of the nuclear family, the twenty-first be the age of the *unclear* family. More and more young people are living through adolescence without the support of a secure family environment. This is not merely a question of 'broken homes'—though these are an increasing element in the lives of young people, and it is predicted that there will be more children in step-families than in nuclear families by 2010—but also of an apparent loss of confidence among parents themselves. According to John Balding, director of Exeter University's schools health education unit,[27] parents often appear 'frightened of their children. They don't know how to give them adequate direction. In order to escape from this, they try to make their children grow up too quickly, and put the responsibility for their actions into the child's hands.'[28] Many commentators note the destructive role of advertainment in this process. Lynne Monck, a secondary school headteacher, commented that media images 'raise expectations about how they should be looking, about the interests that they should be having and what they should be doing. Students are under pressure to match up to the images.'[29] For some, the resultant tension spills over into violence and drug and alcohol abuse. 'Things such as joy-riding and ram-raiding . . . are just the tip of the iceberg of youth alienation and insecurity,' writes Professor Richard Whitfield. 'Children are expected to achieve more—yet many are not getting the parental support they need.'[30]

It is clear that many of the young people caught up in the whirlwind of globalisation and fragmentation in the coming decades will not have a strong, supporting family to turn to. In their struggle for identity—their cry of 'who am I?' so often couched in violent and anti-social terms—they will be thrown alone and unsupported on the mercy of a wider society. All too often, it will be a society with neither the will nor the means to answer.

7. The reinvention of world mission

One final area in which the forces of globalisation and fragmentation will exert significant influence is that of Christian mission. Not only does post-imperialism challenge the link between Christian mission and cultural paternalism, but cross-cultural mission, as it has been practised, is failing for a whole range of reasons to engage the commitment of the emerging generations. Some of the ways in which the transitional generations are challenging traditional views of mission are:

a) They have a different view of 'lostness'

Western imperialism saw European culture as essentially redeemed and redeeming, and non-Western cultures as lost and in need of saving. Post-imperial young people are switching this polarity. They have a deep awareness of the lostness of their own culture, and an increasing appreciation of the redeeming qualities in non-Western cultures, particular those of pre-modern and indigenous religions. Coupled with this, many young people are questioning traditional Christian theologies of judgement and 'lostness'. They are not entirely convinced that every person 'outside of the Church' is condemned to damnation, and are increasingly immune to mission motivated by this concern.

b) They are more drawn to physical service than to evangelism

Just as symbol and community are a language more readily understood by young people than print and text, so action is a more fluent tongue to them than belief. Where Billy Graham might have been the 'Christian icon' of their parents, they are more likely to honour Mother Theresa or—as she embraced the HIV Positive and talked with land-mine victims—Princess Diana. Touch is a strong dynamic among the new generations: there is no mission without real, substantial human contact.

c) They will respond differently to the structures and institutions of mission

In a paper given at the Missions Interlink Forum in Australia in July 1998, Kath Donavan and Ruth Myors note some of the key factors missions agencies need to take account of in working with Generation X and beyond.

They note that GenX are not particularly comfortable in traditionally-structured mission organisations because:

- They are misunderstood—assumed to lack commitment but in fact capable of very deep friendships and commitments.
- They need emotional and spiritual support, carrying a strong awareness of their own vulnerabilities.
- Their view of leadership is egalitarian—they want to be committed not *to* an organisation but with it.
- They are experiential, with a longing for deeper spirituality often unmet in traditional models.
- They look for participative leadership and are empowered by being given scope to run with their vision.[31]

In the comprehensive re-evaluation of Church that the coming decades will bring, it seems unlikely that the traditional view of mission will remain unchallenged. Rather, the post-imperial context of globalisation and fragmentation and the emerging consciousness of Generation X and beyond will combine to redefine and reorder the Church's understanding of its global task. In the transition from Generation X to the Millennials, many of these changes will be accentuated by a shift in historical context. Where GenX have lived with the pessimism of being a pre-millennial generation—a generation born too late to alter history's record of the century in which it has lived, the Millennials will be post-millennial—a generation presented with a new and unformed century on which to make its mark.

Notes

1   Eugene Linden, Legions of the Dispossessed in *Time Magazine*, November 1997.

2   Barrie Taylor, 'Generation X' and Mission, EMA Bulletin, Summer 1998.

3   Robert Beckford, *Jesus is Dread, Black Theology and Black Culture in Britain* (Darton, Longman and Todd: London, 1998).

4   *Ibid*, p.4.

5   H. P. Spees, 'Evangelising Young People in Different Cultures,' study paper for the Convocation of Youth for Christ International, Chicago, USA, 1993.

6   Try it for yourself at http://www.bobmarley.com

7   Tony Lane, *The Lion Concise Book of Christian Thought* (Lion: Oxford 1984).

8   Kosuke Koyami, *Three Mile an Hour God* (SCM: London, 1979), chapter 1.

9   H. P. Spees, *op.cit*.

10   *Faith in the City: A Call for Action by Church and Nation* (Church House Publishing: London, 1985).

11   Oliver James, *Britain on the Couch* (Arrow Books: London, 1988),p.21.For an extract, see http://cgi.pathfinder.com/time/magazine/1977/int/970922/essay.puting-britai.htm/

12   *Ibid*.

13   For background and links to Dr Campolo's work, see http://www.eastern.edu/centres/eape/

14   Tony Campolo, video interview, 'Preparing to Parent Teenagers Seminar', Youth for Christ, 1996.

15   Mike Riddell, *Godzone—A Guide to the Travels of the Soul* Lion: Oxford, 1992, pp. 14ff.

16   Oliver James, op cit, p. 26

17   J. Richard Middleton and Brian J. Walsh, op.cit, p.77.

18   Ushio Amagatsu, leader of Japanese dance group Sankai Juku, quoted in 'The Aliens have Landed', *The Independent*, London, 15 January. 1999.

19   Rupert Cornwell, 'Will this child inherit his earth?' , *The*

Independent, 9 July 1998. Visit the Survival International homepage at http://www.survival.org.uk/about.htm

20 *Ibid*

21 *The Financial Times*, London, 16 July. 1996, quoted by John Abbot, The 20th Century Learning Initiative, seminar presentation, 1998.

22 Rachel Johnnson, 'The Picture Still Looks Grim', *The Financial Times*, London, January 1994

23 Ibid.

24 Matthew Connelly and Paul Kennedy, 'Must It Be The Rest Against The West?' *The Atlantic Monthly*, December 1994

25 Cited in Matthew Connelly and Paul Kennedy, *op.cit.*

26 John Grigg, 'What makes a great leader?', *The Times*, London, 9 February, 1999.

27 http://www.info.ex.ac.uk/~dregis/sheu.html

28 Young People in 1992: A survey by the Schools Health Education Unit of Exeter University, reported in *The Sunday Times*, January 1993.

29 'Britain's Children Showing Signs of Stress', *The Sunday Times*, January 1993

30 Ibid

31 Quoted in *EMA Bulletin*, autumn 1998, from a chapter by Myors and Donavan in *Too Valuable to Lose: the causes and cures of missionary attrition*, W.D. Taylor, ed., (William Carey Library, 1997).

12

GODS 'R' US
Post-Christian Spirituality

After years in the popular wilderness, God is staging a come-back . . . Re-appraisal for the spiritual life is coming from the least likely quarters: scientific, secular and popular.

The Face, January 1997[1]

Is there any truth in the cliché that today's youth is fearfully searching for signs and portents, miracles, gurus and the big idea . . ? Even the most ungodly clubbers now chill out to the sound of Gregorian chants and wear magic rune symbols on their chests.

Helen Chappell[2]

Spirits in a material world

With a long history of radical humanism and a public school system built exclusively and deliberately on the values of *laicité* (secularism), France might well be described as one of the world's least believing nations. All the more surprising then that belief in God, and in the non-material realm, remains a strong and persistent feature in the lives of French young people. In a nation in which weekly church attendance has plunged since 1945 from close to 80% of the population to less than 14%, young people cling all the same to a sense of God and an interest in spirituality. In 1994, the magazine *Phosphore*[3] interviewed a representative national sample of fifteen to twenty-year-olds to find out just how deep such beliefs run. Their findings confirm that, while the Church may be outmoded, God is in the house. 55% thought the existence of God certain or likely compared to just 38% unlikely or impossible. 40% attributed the creation of the world to 'a greater power'. Asked what they expected to experience after death, only 16% believed that there was nothing. Among the rest there was belief in eternal life, reincarnation and bodily resurrection—but a full 50% expressed the view that 'there is something but we don't know what'.[4]

The *Phosphore* survey gave a clear signal that belief persists, but that it is less and less connected to traditional, established or orthodox creeds. Of the 55% who rated the existence of God 'certain or likely', 31% qualified this God as 'present within each one of us' while only 19% could believe in God as 'a being who has spoken to humankind in history'.

Commenting on these outcomes, sociologist Francoise Champion linked the preference for an 'inner God' to deep cultural changes amounting to a new spirit of the age. 'What we look for today is personal experience,' she says. 'What counts is to feel something. This new way of dealing with faith is not restricted to the young.'[5] Nor is it restricted to France—these findings resonate with parallel evidence right across Western culture. There is a blossoming of spirituality among the young people of Generation X and beyond, but for many this goes hand in hand with a rejection of the creeds of the established church. It is in this sense that the newly-formed cultures of the twenty-first century are post-Christian.

Definitions

The world of Generation X and beyond will be post-Christian in the sense that:

1. The primary influence on popular spirituality is no longer orthodox Christianity.
2. In its place, new generic spiritualities are emerging which prioritise personal experience, pluralism and self-made creeds.
3. The influence of these perspectives is pervasive, touching many who would not call themselves 'religious' and sparking a revival in spirituality.
4. The new emphasis on spirituality will shape the way individuals choose and express a faith, but will also impact the ways in which popular culture perceives and judges the Christian Church.

Before we look at some of the implications of the post-Christian spirituality of youth, it is important that we understand more fully where this influence has come from. We will do this by examining three separate strands in our recent cultural history; each representing an area of search and exploration; each, in its way, giving rise to new spiritual life.

New gods

Post-Christian spirituality is above all else a symptom of the wide and long-established decline of the Church's influence in the West. For centuries the term 'Christendom' described the 'forms of Christian civilisation which have given Western peoples their spiritual values, their moral standards, and their conception of a divine law from which all human laws ultimately derive their validity and their sanction'.[6] But such a close connection of faith and culture is a thing of the past. As

David Bjork has written, we now stand in the wake of 'two hundred years of progressive secularisation during which the distinctively Christian institutions and social standards have been gradually eliminated. Many contemporary missiologists and sociologists have used the term post-Christian to identify this trend in contemporary Western European culture.'[7] This decline flies in the face of the global picture, in which the Christian faith is still in the ascendant. 'While continuing to flourish in the fertile cultural fields to which the faith was exported,' says Mike Riddell, 'Christianity has steadily diminished in those lands which were the "sending nations" . . . The one massive gap in the Church's expertise is how to do mission in the post-Christian West.'[8]

In one sense, none of this is news. The decline of Christendom has been observed and commented on for much of the twentieth century. What is newer, and to many a surprise, is the blossoming, in this context, of popular spirituality. Where the harsh, dry conditions and hard ground of secularisation might have been expected to produce little in terms of spiritual growth, they have seen a remarkable flowering of personal faith. Jacob Needleman and David Applebaum, Professors of Philosophy at San Francisco State University and State University College, New Paltz respectively, are in no doubt as to the origin of this spiritual awakening:

In almost every area of our culture, the realisation is dawning that material progress and scientific achievement cannot of themselves lead us towards an understanding of the meaning of our lives . . . Our modern contemporary civilisation is characterised by its fascination with the technological application of scientific discovery and its neglect of those aspects of our nature that require other kinds of perceptions, other kinds of "food". These parts of our mind, these aspects of ourselves, are starving, and if they die, we will die with them. This is not speculation: it is an obvious truth that we are all beginning to sense.[9]

Writing from a Christian perspective, John Drane makes the same observation, 'Rapidly increasing numbers are finding it possible to believe in reincarnation, spirit guides and extra-terrestrials and all sorts of other esoteric ideas,' he says, 'It certainly means that these people are spiritually open as no other generation in living memory has been.'[10] In the ruins of modernity, with the dream of a scientific utopia in tatters, spiritual shoots are growing with unexpected strength.

New science

A second source of inspiration for the post-Christian spiritual rebirth comes, ironically, from science itself. Even as millions of young people have questioned the scientific account of life and meaning, scientists have been exploring the boundaries of belief and truth. Research in quantum physics and related fields has undermined confidence in the materialist / empirical worldview, and scientists working at the very limits of human knowledge have found themselves standing on common ground with those holding a more spiritual, pre-enlightenment view. 'It has taken scientists until the second half of the twentieth century to prove what we have known all along,' writes one native-American commentator, 'we are all related. Not just human beings, but four-legged and winged brothers and sisters, as well as those who crawl.'[11]

While general science has opened the door, if tentatively, to the possibility of faith, there are specific scientists moving much faster to embrace a spiritual worldview. Biologist Rupert Sheldrake, who has held senior posts at both Harvard and Cambridge Universities, is just one of the many scientists who is forging a path away from the mechanistic worldview towards more traditional, spiritual concepts.

A lot of harm was done in the West by splitting apart science and religion in the seventeenth century. Science became very limited in its focus to mechanical, material things, and religion became very introverted; it became very concerned just with the human spirit and with morality . . . In most traditional cultures, these are not separated in that way . . . I think that as science emerges from this narrow, mechanistic phase that it has been in and we move to a broader vision, a new kind of connection between the realms of science and spirituality becomes possible.[12]

Sheldrake's personal journey takes in a fascination with Eastern mysticism, and his work lays foundations for the 'new science'—an approach which, far from rejecting spiritual experience, provides it with a context and rationale. His theories of morphic resonance represent an exploration of the connectedness of all nature, and an objective apologetic for monism, the belief that 'all is one'.

Through the work of scientists such as Sheldrake, and notably the physicist Fritjof Capra, the deadlock between science and faith is being broken down. Spiritual searchers are being encouraged to believe that science may not after all have written the gods out of history.[13]

New Age

Many of those embracing new expressions of spirituality have done so under the umbrella of the New Age movement. Born in the late 1960s as the 'Age of Aquarius', the New Age movement peaked in the mid 1980s as thousands of young and not-so-young Westerners signed up for courses in spirituality and self-actualisation. The spark that ignited this movement, at first in America and later through-out Western culture, was the belief that the planet was mov-ing from the age of Pisces—marked by the dualities of good vs evil, male vs female, spirit vs body, humanity vs nature etc., to the age of Aquarius—marked by harmony in these and all other matters. A long-held view among astrologers, the division of human history into astrological ages of approximately 2,000 years was promoted by psychologist Carl Jung and became a popular view in the 1960s. The age of Pisces, in this view, had begun in AD1, and would give way to Aquarius some time in 1997. The Aquarian Age used the language of astrology, and the fast-approaching end of the millennium, to give voice to a 'cosmic evolutionary opti-mism'[14] that had begun to surface in the 1960s, not least in the writings of Teillhard de Chardin.

A priest, scientist and philosopher, Teillhard ploughed what was then a lone furrow in bringing these disparate fields together. The closing words of his *The Future of Man* now read like a classic New Age text, but in the 1960s they were a radical new faith looking for a name and a home.

And then will be the end. Like a vast tide the Being will have dominated the trembling of all beings. The extraordinary adventure of the world will have ended in the bosom of a tran-quil ocean, of which however each drop will still be conscious of being itself.[15]

By giving this optimism a name and a focus, the 'Age of Aquarius' created a platform of credibility for all things alternative, and at break-neck speed a movement grew up in which the only thing you *couldn't* do was stay the same. The watershed publication in this explosion of new thinking was Marilyn Ferguson's *The Aquarian Conspiracy* in 1980. Fer-guson used the term conspiracy in a loose and positive sense to describe her feeling that there was an unspoken connect-edness among a whole range of new groups, communities, therapies and theories emerging in America. It was essentially after her book was published that the term 'New Age movement' became current.

Across the Atlantic, author Jean-Luc Porquet observed the early growth of this same movement in the French context. 'Suddenly, we saw dynamic young executives walking on hot coals', he writes, 'and gurus affirming that they were the reincarnated inhabitants of the lost island of Atlantis.'[16] Porquet is quick to point out that in France, as elsewhere, this first 'New Age' movement has now given way to a second, looser, more diverse period.

> All this quickly went out of fashion, but a second, more discreet New Age arose in its place . . . With neither a leader nor single organisation, this New Age is a kind of network of networks in which you find journals, conferences, publications, specialist bookshops, music and, most of all—in this ideal promotional environment—a vast array of training courses.[17]

This second-wave New Age movement has grown away from a specific belief in a new astrological age to embrace a more general commitment to spirituality, personal fulfil-ment and self-actualisation. In this sense, the New Age movement has become part of the wider shift in our culture towards a post-Christian spirituality.

New Age thinking has contributed to this shift, and many people remain committed to core New Age ideas, but it is a mistake to see post-Christian spirituality as purely a product of the New Age movement. While the movement itself will continue to influence thousands, the wider cultural shift toward exploratory and experiential spirituality will impact millions, and will be a key factor in shaping Western culture

in the coming decades. Post-Christian spirituality will be a
factor in the lives of young people long after the term New
Age has dropped out of our speech, and thousands have
deserted the movement in bitter disappointment at an age
of harmony that never arrived.

Unconnectable Jesus

These three factors then, the West's search for new gods, new
science and a new age, have been primary influences on the
wave of post-Christian spirituality we are now seeing. At the
heart of this spiritual renaissance there is a cruel irony for the
Christian Church. On the one hand it heralds the return to
spiritual pursuits that the Church, in the face of growing secularisation, materialism and humanism, has longed for. At
its heart is the recognition that there is reality beyond the
material; that empiricism is not the final answer; that the
'soul' is as real as the body. It represents, in essence, a recovery of the supernatural. But on the other hand, this new-
found desire for faith among the young sees the Christian
Church as an integral part of the very modernity it rejects.
'Before Christians get too excited about the renewed interest
in religion,' writes Mike Riddell, 'it is well to note that the
emerging culture's exploration of spirituality is in many ways
a reaction against institutional Christianity as it has been
experienced in the West.'[18] John Drane sounds much the
same warning, 'Christianity is very firmly perceived as part
of the old order,' he writes, 'and therefore something to be
discarded rather than trusted for the future.'[19]

This is not to say that there is no scope for Christian
growth in such a context. A spirituality which is post-
Christian is not by definition anti-Christian—it is 'post' in
the sense of 'going beyond'. Post-Christian young people
are not dismissing any possibility of encounter with the

Christian God, but they are rejecting the forms and formulae in which they have seen faith in that God expressed. This ambivalence is captured by Douglas Coupland in his reaction to the output of American Christian radio stations. 'I did not deny the existence of Jesus was real to these people,' he says, 'it was merely that I was cut off from their experience in a way that was never connectable.'[20]

Whatever the future holds for Christian mission in Western culture, it will require of us that we overcome, for millions of young people, this perception of an 'unconnectable Jesus'. This will mean making connections with the very spirituality that has, in its post-Christian pilgrimage, rejected what it knows of Christ. A starting point for this process lies in a fuller exploration of the nature and key themes of popular spirituality among young people. The five themes outlined below by no means exhaust the exploration of post-Christian spirituality, but they each provide a starting point for a fuller understanding of it.

1. Can't believe it's not Buddha—the exploration of non-Western faiths

There are clear parallels between the dynamics of the emerging spirituality and the central ideas of Eastern faiths—Buddhism, Hinduism and their many, many mystical spin-offs. Westerners disillusioned with their own society, and unconvinced of Christianity's capacity to heal it, have taken their search for enlightenment East. Film director Martin Scorsese, responsible for the 1998 biography of the Dalai Lama *Kundun,* explains this attraction:

I can't talk about the nature of man because I'm not a philosopher. I just know that what I was taught in church and what I was taught on the street are two different things. Somehow one has to win out. That's the same thing the Tibetans are talking about: compassion, love, kindness and tolerance. Ultimately, this film is about non-violence and I've seen too much that was the other way.[21]

Scorsese is not alone in failing to see '*compassion, love, kindness and tolerance*' in the dealings of the Christian Church. Throughout the West, young people are finding in the Eastern tradition a purity and detachment which they believe Christianity to have lost. The faith of the West, by contrast, they view as complicit in the very violence from which they seek release.

Among the heroes and role models finding favour in a new generation are monks like Shi Yanzzi, a master of Shoalin Kung Fu[22] recently despatched from deepest China to set up a Shoalin temple in London. Shi Yanzzi and his colleagues have been featured in *The Face* and *Esquire* magazines, as well as drawing huge crowds to martial arts displays demonstrating both physical and spiritual excellence. Grace Bradberry of *The Times* describes the lifestyle that appears so attractive to a young, Western audience: 'In a typical day he spends two hours meditating and three hours studying the Buddhist scripture, as well as devoting six hours to kung fu training.' Of the resultant martial arts displays, she writes, 'The aura of spiritual calm is what makes the performance so remarkable.'[23]

Somehow disillusionment with the West has become disillusionment with the faith from which it grew, and only the non-Western offers hope. As John Drane points out,

One of the key things that I hear people saying is that they think the church is irrelevant—they actually say it is unspiritual, that if you want spirituality, the last place to go to is the church . . . Many people seem to believe that the church is not a place where you find spirituality anyway. It's a place where you'll find hair-splitting theology.'[24]

2. Wanting to be Indian—the embracing of pre-Western faiths

Alongside contemporary non-Western expressions of faith, the richest source of inspiration for the emerging post-Christian spirituality has been the pre-Western faith of indigenous peoples. The motivation is the same—a genuine disillusionment with the Western 'project'—but the prescription is different. Instead of looking beyond their own borders to faiths expressed in other regions of the world, Western young people are looking to their own roots, and asking what expressions of faith existed in their own lands before the arrival of Christianity, science and the modern worldview.

> Many people are searching for a deeper spiritual engagement with the world and feel a hunger unmet by the teachings and services of traditional religious institutions. Some have begun to take an interest in Native American spiritual practices, and one can easily find workshops and lectures offering Indian rituals and ceremonies to non-Indian people.[25]

A similar assessment could be made in other parts of the world. Whether the Indian tribes of North, Central and South America, the Aboriginal peoples of Australia and New Zealand or the pagan Celts of Europe, the religions of 'first peoples' are experiencing a remarkable, worldwide revival. Lecturer John Barry Ryan suggests some of the elements of native spirituality that appeal to the post-modern mind. 'These rituals are communal, earthy and experiential, with group involvement in rites that appeal to the senses,' he writes. 'This contrasts strongly with an individualistic approach to overly intellectualised worship forms that leaves the participant alienated.'[26]

Canadian artist Dale Stonechild describes the very

personal way in which he is rediscovering the power and value of his own native background.

> When I was a boy, whenever I asked, "Why?" my grandmother and the old people would answer by telling stories. These stories related the marvellous exploits of many wondrous creatures and beings. All the stories had a moral lesson. They taught me how to behave, and they taught me about nature and life on Mother Earth ... After my old people died, I forgot these stories. Now, I am returning to them ... reconnecting with the teachings of these stories.[27]

Native religions did not rely on propositional truth, theology or preaching, but on community, ritual and story—strong themes in the post-modern worldview. Neither could they be approached from an individualised position. 'Indian religions are not something one can convert to, as one might to Christianity, by adopting a set of beliefs or principles,' writes Myke Johnson. 'Indian religions are built upon systems of relationships.'[28]

Looking to the past is one very clear way in which Western people disillusioned with the present and nervous of the future are seeking inspiration. Young people at odds with modernity and unsure just what postmodernity will bring look to premodernity for clues. There are many questions to be asked about just what they find in their search; about just how transferable and adaptable these religions are; about whether it is even possible for Western, predominantly white young people to indwell these ancient stories in any meaningful way. But even acknowledging such questions, we would be fools to ignore the deeply-felt needs that this resurgence of native faiths reveals. Whatever the future holds, there is something in these stories and rituals, in this simpler more reverential worldview, that is deeply appealing to the young of the twenty-first-century West. A Church which ignores their voice is a Church trapped in the twentieth century, and destined for the dustbin of history.

3. Eco-puritans of Wandsworth—recovering reverence for the earth

A third significant theme in the post-Christian spirituality of our age, and one which overlaps considerably with the appeal of native religions, is that of sacred ecology. So great is the swing towards environmental awareness among the young that it has ceased to be simply a matter of lifestyle and sustainability, but has spilled over into spirituality and become an issue of faith.

When journalist Paul Vallely went to visit anti-development protestors who had illegally occupied a site at Gargoyle Wharf in London in 1995, he found a temporary community bound together not only by an immediate sense of purpose—to stop a planned shops, apartments and petrol station development—but by a long-term, underlying commitment to the integrity of the environment. 'In a post-Christian age, where ecology has become the nearest thing we have to a shared religion,' he wrote, 'the Eco-Puritans of Wandsworth are not so far removed from the Christian Puritans of the seventeenth century as might be imagined.'[29]

If there is any one theme that runs through most contemporary expressions of post-Christian spirituality, whether inspired by Buddhism, Celtic paganism or New Age eclecticism, it is this theme of the sacredness of nature. Reverence for the earth—respect for non-human creatures; for the natural world; for the elements of fire, water, earth and air—is a strand so woven into these new faith expressions that it would be all but impossible to imagine them without it. The Western way is rejected because of its destruction of the Earth. Christianity is rejected because of its traditional interpretation of the Genesis mandate 'to rule and subdue' as a licence to dominate, exploit and destroy. To the new Eco-puritans the Church, for the most part, is the enemy.

One powerful expression of this theme, particularly strong among those whose roots, if not their current practice, are in orthodox Christianity, is the 'creation-centred spirituality' associated with former Dominican priest Matthew Fox. From being a radical voice on the fringes of Catholic theology, Fox, now expelled from the Dominican order, has moved in recent years to being probably *the* voice at the heart of the new eco-orthodoxy. He rejects the notion of the fallenness of the natural world and speaks instead of 'original blessing'—the essential goodness of the creation. His Jesus is the 'cosmic Christ', identified with and at times inseparable from mother Earth. 'Though Fox affirms belief in the historical Jesus,' writes Mitchell Pacwa, SJ, 'he considers the Cosmic Christ to be a "third nature" in addition to the divine and human nature. By saying it is the "I am" in every creature, the Cosmic Christ is identified with creation. The earth is called the Cosmic Christ.'[30] Ritual is of great importance, and centres on the cosmic mass, when the Christian Eucharist is re-imagined in terms of the salvation of mother Earth. Communion itself, in this context, becomes 'the eating and drinking of the wounded earth'.[31] Fox has recently dialogued with Rupert Sheldrake to produce a book *Natural Grace: Dialogues on Science and Spirituality*. 'Essentially he is trying to recover a sense of spirituality in nature,' Sheldrake explains, 'that it's not just something inside, or to do with morality and sin. It's to do with the whole of nature. The divine presence in the sky, in the earth, in our experience of nature all around us.'[32]

Fox and Sheldrake co-habit the overlap between Christianity and a post-Christian approach, but they are not alone in their embracing of creation-centred spirituality. There are

those who have retained stronger links with Christian orthodoxy but are nonetheless working to recover a more reverential view of the created order, while others whose roots are
entirely outside the Christian faith community share the same
goal. For some, sacred ecology is the very heart and soul of
their faith; for others it is a low-profile element, pervading
belief but never quite breaking the surface. In either case, and
for millions of young people the world over, a faith which does
not deal in respectful terms with the non-human creation, and
look in some measure to the healing of the earth, will have no
place in the twenty-first century worldview.

4. I have to *feel* it—the primacy of personal experience

A fourth theme which emerges as a common thread in post-
Christian spirituality, despite the variance and diversity of
its expressions, is that of the personalisation of religious
experience. Just as Teillhard de Chardin anticipated much
that was to come in terms of New Age optimism, so the psychologist Carl Jung, who died in 1961, foresaw the radical
shifting of faith from the public, corporate, institutional and
communal domains to the realm of personal experience.

> The seat of faith . . . is not consciousness but spontaneous reli-
> gious experience . . . It will always remain doubtful whether
> what metaphysics and theology call God and the gods is the
> real ground of these experiences. The question is idle, actually,
> and answers itself by reason of the subjectively overwhelming
> numinosity of the experience.[33]

Jung's thought was widely popularised in the 1960s, and
became foundational to the notion that spirituality was
primarily about personal experience, measured not in terms

of adherence to given rules of belief or behaviour, but subjectively, in terms of the depth of the experience itself.

For Jung—and for the generations who have followed him, many knowing neither his name nor his ideas—spiritual experience is not the means by which faith achieves its end, it is an end in itself. The God we reach out for does not exist objectively, separate from us and outside of our experience, but is contained, somehow, in the great ocean of the unconscious mind. Thus post-Christian spirituality is predominantly inward-looking. Where there is a focus on healing and harmony, on justice and compassion, this is the outworking of the inner experience. The healing of the cosmos begins with the healing of the person.

5. I have to *use* it—the necessity of a practicable spirituality

One final area in which post-Christian spirituality marks a departure from contemporary Christian experience is in its practicability. Whether in the rituals of native faith, in the techniques of Eastern mysticism or in the diverse experiences of the New Age, there is in popular spirituality an increasing focus on doing. Techniques of meditation, prayer beads and wheels; repeated individual and corporate rituals; breathing exercises; Tai Chi; inversion therapy; chanting; silent sitting— these and thousands of other techniques on offer invite spiritual devotees not to believe something but to do something.

Many post-Christian spiritualities do not revolve around regular attendance at some public assembly or act of worship, but around a regular—often daily—cycle of personal spiritual exercises. More often than not this will be a cycle or pattern that can be woven unobtrusively into the busy patterns of contemporary urban life: bite-sized chunks of spiritual experience to offer brief pools of stillness in the frenetic rush; moments of sanity in a world gone mad; oases of refreshment for the urban desert. The practitioner of such exercises becomes responsible for her own spirituality, sensitive to the inner rhythms of her own experience, the arbiter of her own spiritual journey. 'One of the major reasons for the rapid growth of the New Age in recent years,' writes John Drane, 'is the need felt by many people for some kind of hands-on symbols, rituals and experiences that will hold out the promise of putting them in tune with the mystery that is God.'[34] Christianity, by contrast, even though it has examples of many of these techniques in its own long and diverse history, has tended in the twentieth century to focus on belief—to be a religion of propositional truth. This has been especially true of the Protestant denominations, but is often also true of Catholics, who experience the rituals and routines of their church not as dynamic personal exercises but as the mumbled, all-too-familiar patterns of spiritual wallpaper. Spiritual seekers visiting a Christian church may be offered the opportunity to observe and to listen, and may be invited at some stage to give assent—but they are unlikely to be given new techniques to 'try out'. Nor will there be a take-away bag of faith and practice to sustain them through the ensuing days. There may be sound theological reasons for this—the Church may wish to hold onto the notion that belief, in some form, must precede experience. But while it is doing so, the spiritual searcher will simply go elsewhere—and who knows how many might come into belief, given a practicable and personal entry-point?

Notes

1 *The Face*, January 1997, quoted in Pete Greig, 'E Generation', *Compass Magazine*, spring 1998. Adapted from the forthcoming book *The Awakening Cry*.

2 Helen Chappell, 'It's hip to be holy', *New Statesman and Society*, 8 September 1995.

3 http://www.phosphore.com/common/info/index.html

4 '15–20 ans croyez-vous en Dieu?', *Phosphore Magazine*, December 1994.

5 Quoted in *Phosphore Magazine*.

6 Christopher Dawson, *The Historic Reality of Christian Culture* (Harper Torchbooks: New York, 1965).

7 David Bjork, *A Model for the Analysis of Incarnational Ministry in Post-Christendom Lands*, PhD research (Fuller Theological Seminary).

8 Mike Riddell, *Threshold of the Future—Reforming the Church in the Post-Christian West* (SPCK: London, 1998), p. 12.

9 Jacob Needleman and David Applebaum, *Real Philosophy, An Anthology of the Universal Search for Meaning* (Arkana (Penguin), 1990), p. 12.

10 John Drane, *What is the New Age Saying to the Church?* (Marshall Pickering: London, 1991), p. 239.

11 Alankentkataxkwe (Star Dancer), 'Lenapé Spirituality', Internet article at http://www.geocities.com/Athens/forum/4438/spirit.html

12 Rupert Sheldrake interviewed by Ken Weathersby, *Hootenanny Magazine*, 1995, Internet article at http://www.bway.net/~drkeith/hoot/3/sheldrake.html

13 For a further exploration of the relationship between science and faith, see Roger Forster and Paul Marston, *Reason, Science and Faith* (Monarch: Crowborough, 1999).

14 Jefferis Kent Peterson, 'The New Age Movement: The Self as God', Internet article at http://www.cbl.org/scholarC/Newage.html

15 Teilhard de Chardin, *The Future of Man*, conclusion, quoted in Tony Lane, *The Lion Concise Book of Christian Thought* (Lion: Oxford, 1984).

16 Jean-Luc Porquet, 'Le New Age, religion fast food', *Phosphore Magazine*, December 1994. Porquet is the author of *La France des Mutants, voyage au coeur du New Age* (Editions Flammarion, 1994).

17 Jean-Luc Porquet, 'Le New Age, religion fast food', *Phosphore Magazine*, December 1994.

18 Mike Riddell, *op. cit.*, p. 115.

19 John Drane, *Evangelism for a New Age: Creating Churches for the Next Century* (Marshall Pickering: London, 1994), p. 15.

20 Douglas Coupland, *Life After God*, p. 183, quoted in John Crowdis, 'Facing the Hurricane, A look at Society and Church', Internet article http://www.presbycan.ca/pccmall/pphiles/GenXPP.html

21 Martin Scorsese quoted by Lesley O'Toole, 'Into Battle for A Man of Peace', *The Times*, London, 31 March 1998.

22 See http://www.webcom.com/~shaolin/

23 Grace Bradberry, 'Monks with a lethal habit', *The Times*, London, 31 March 1998.

24 John Drane interviewed by Wendy Beech, Youth for Christ, April 1996.

25 Myke Johnson, *Wanting to be Indian—When Spiritual Teaching Turns Into Cultural Theft* (Respect Inc., PO Box 2516, Boston, MA 02130, USA, 1995).

26 John Barry Ryan, 'Listening to Native Americans—Making Peace with the Past for the Future', Internet article.

27 Dale Stonechild, in *First Nations Gallery Guide* (Royal Saskatchewan Museum, Canada).

28 Myke Johnson, *op. cit.*

29 Paul Vallely, 'England's gentle revolutionaries', *The Independent*, 27 May 1996.

30 Mitchell Pacwa, SJ, 'Catholicism for the New Age: Matthew Fox and Creation-Centred Spirituality', *Christian Research Journal*, autumn 1992, p. 14.

31 Matthew Fox, *The Coming of the Cosmic Christ* (Harper and Row: San Francisco, 1988), quoted in the *Journal of the Christian Research Institute*, PO Box 500, San Juan Capistrano, CA 92693, USA.

32 Rupert Sheldrake interviewed by Ken Weathersby, *Hootenanny Magazine*, 1995. Internet article at http://www.bway.net/~drkeith/hoot/3/sheldrake.html

33 Carl G. Jung, *The Undiscovered Self, 1957, 1958*, quoted at http://www.geocities.com/Athens/Acropolis/3976/Jung.html

34 John Drane, *op. cit.*

13

KHARMA-GEDDON
Living with Post-Christian Spirituality

We talked for more than an hour. He seemed to have been evangelised more often than Nicky Gumbel's hairdresser. "I am incredibly impressed with the person of Jesus", he confided, "but there is absolutely nothing in Christianity or the church that attracts or inspires me." I searched his face for a trace of cynicism. I found nothing but sadness there. I asked if he would help me build a church for people like him and he agreed.

Pete Greig[1]

This hunger for spirituality does not today, perhaps for the first time in many centuries, cause people to come to the churches. If . . . we live in the midst of a time of genuine spiritual search analogous to the Great Awakening, how do we communicate the riches of our spiritual heritage to a generation not interested in being in communication with what churches do?

Loren Mead[2]

In 1835, a seventeen-year-old in Germany included the following words in a school-leaving essay.

Union with Christ consists in the most intimate communion with Him, in having Him before our eyes and in our hearts, and being so filled with the highest love for Him, that at the same time we turn our hearts to our brothers whom He has closely bound to us, and for whom He also sacrificed Himself.[3]

Tame words—standard fare from a young Christian with a passionate faith and a good handle on religious jargon. But hollow words, and strange when you realise that they were written by Karl Marx. For those concerned with the discipling of young lives in the building of the 'once and future church'.[4] Marx's words stand as an urgent reminder that the stakes are high. The task of passing on the Christian witness amounts to more than teaching the young a few religious words and eliciting a programmed response. Marx may well have been happy at seventeen to 'talk the talk' of religious faith, but the experiences that shaped his life and the deep truths that motivated him were drawn from other fountains—and bore a very different fruit.

Faith that lasts is about more than superficial belief, it is about deep experiences; significant relationships; strong convictions; the shaping of a worldview. Unless faith is deeply rooted in the lives of the young, they will not carry it with them into their later adult years—and the Church will not be re-rooted in the cultures they create. The crisis of the Western Church at the end of the twentieth century could be summed up in this one failing—it has not engaged deeply enough with the cultures of the young. The need to embrace change; to create structures and models of church and community that resonate with the transitional generations is urgent.

The post-Christian spiritualities evident in the transitional generations threaten many strongly-held views of the twentieth century Church—but equally, many of the themes and nuances of these spiritualities are present in that same Church's history. After two thousand years of

growth, diversity, experimentation, discovery and experience, the Christian Church has a vast store of spiritual
expression available to it. The problem has been that much
of this expression remains locked in the store-room, and
that so little of it has been on display of late in the Church's
shop windows. The issue is not that the Church has no
future, but that it has no future without change.

Among missiologists and cultural analysts across the
denominational spectrum, a consensus is emerging that significant engagement with the emerging twenty-first-century
cultures will take the Church on a journey well beyond the
boundaries of its present experience—and certainly beyond
its comfort zones. Writing in the North American context in
1998, George Barna expresses this consensus in stark terms:

> At the risk of sounding like an alarmist, I believe the church in
> America has no more than five years—perhaps even less—to
> turn itself around and begin to affect the culture, rather than be
> affected by it . . . we have no more than a half-decade to turn
> things around.[5]

The Church we have known in the twentieth century
stands on the threshold of the future much as a grain of
wheat might stand before a ploughed field. It has within
itself the genetic riches necessary for a bumper crop, but as
Oscar Romero has written, 'The harvest comes because the
grain of wheat dies. The earth allows itself to be sacrificed,
broken; only in being broken does it produce the harvest.'[6]

It is appropriate to remind ourselves, at this point, of the
huge significance of the transitional generations, Generation X and beyond, to this crisis. These generations represent the last young adult generation of the twentieth
century and the first of the twenty-first. By the year 2020,
they will constitute the entire working population of the

Western world. Everyone under sixty who might or might not join your church at that date will be shaped by the GenX/Millennial experience—in varying degrees post-industrial, post-literate, post-modern, post-imperial and post-Christian. Thus to begin now to consider how the Church might adapt to this experience is not to enter into a peripheral concern for youth ministry, but to weigh up the very future of the Church. There is no response to the future which is not a response to GenX and the Millennials.

Where the Church is responding, where it is recognising and engaging with the post-Christian spiritualities of our times, it is sowing seeds of hope for the years ahead. Not only is there a very real possibility that the Church will discover, in the coming decades, new ways of expressing its life and faith that will appeal to post-Christian young people, but there are signs even now of such expressions emerging. These do not come from any one denomination, theology or stream but are emerging in many branches of the Christian family as young leaders respond to the post-Christian spiritualities we have identified; exploring those aspects of their faith which are non-Western, pre-Western, ecological, experiential and practicable. Many of these new expressions are small and faltering and some will peter out before they have had time to amount to anything, but others will gain strength and grow to become, for thousands, new points of entry into Christian faith and practice. Only time will prove which are, in embryonic form, the mainstream Christian expressions of the twenty-first century.

1. Alternative worship—a grassroots movement

Across Great Britain, in Australia and New Zealand and in certain parts of Europe, a loose network of experimental worship communities is emerging, with a very real commitment to embrace the post-Christian generations. Often highly technological, these groups create worship which is visual and participative, which creates and discovers new Christian rituals and which recaptures something of the ecological commitment inherent in the biblical narrative.[7] The most widely known of these experiments was the 'Nine O'Clock Service' in Sheffield—the subject of much press attention around the 'fall' of its leader, Chris Brain. Before sinking into a mire of sexual intrigue and manipulative leadership, the Nine O'Clock Service was a remarkable experiment in post-Christian spirituality, encompassing sound and vision, ritual, community and an over-arching ecological reverence. Other groups with a mercifully lower profile, such as the Late Late Service in Glasgow and Grace in London, have been able to continue these explorations, and are creating a diverse range of models for worship, community and teaching. Their number fast growing, most of these groups are exploring the forms of post-literate learning described in Chapter 7, and appealing directly to the concerns of a post-Christian spirituality. Often they are 'fringe' or 'sister' groups to an established congregation or parish, fitting the definition of a 'licensed experiment'. For the most part they are small projects, learning as they go, making mistakes and struggling to stay on track. Some are dipping their toes into post-modern waters, others wading waist deep, others still diving deep and staying under. Their shared commitment is to ask what it will mean for the Christian faith to be rerooted in the emerging cultures of the transitional generations. As such they are a measure of the Western Church's potential for rebirth.

2. Ancient paths—the rediscovery of Celtic faith

A much wider movement, touching both Catholic and Protestant denominations and appealing both to old and young is the re-emergence of Celtic spirituality. Championed by such writers as Ian Bradley, Michael Mitton, Esther de Waal and David Adam, and popularised through monastic and lay groups such as the Iona and Northumbria Communities, the Celtic worldview strikes a resonant chord with the concerns of post-Christian spirituality. It embraces a love of nature and a passion for its wild and elemental forces, a love of art and poetry, a love of story as the primary means of learning, respect for the role and ministry of women, a rejection of any supposed boundary between the sacred and the secular, a place both for personal devotion and its communal expression, an emphasis on the dynamic experience of intimacy with God. Esther de Waal says of these ancient ways:

> The Celtic journey I am describing . . . is unlike any other journey that I know. Its shape and its end are different, as are the songs I sing while I journey, the company I keep on the road. I have been brought into contact with the visual and the non-verbal, confronted by the power of image and symbol. I have found myself thinking about God as a poet, an artist, drawing us all into his great work of art. I have been taken beyond the rational and intellectual and cerebral for this world touches the springs of my imagination.[8]

For many the rediscovery of the Celtic way represents the return to an authentic, ancient faith. In the same way that many native spiritualities are seen as immune from the corruption of the West, so Celtic Christianity, as a pre-modern form, is ascribed a certain purity. Ian Bradley, for instance, disassociates the Celtic church from the 'evangelism as conquest' style so often associated with modernity. He writes:

The approach of the Celtic missionaries was essentially gentle and sensitive. They sought to live alongside the people with whom they wanted to share the good news of Christ, to understand and respect their beliefs and not to dominate or culturally condition them.[9]

The rebirth of the Celtic church is attributed by many commentators to the close parallels between pre-modern and post-modern Britain. 'Looking back at the Celtic church gives me great heart and vision for the future.' writes Michael Mitton. 'It is as though God is alerting us to the fact that he has done the impossible before in these lands. He has broken into a society that was culturally confused and riddled with spiritual uncertainty and superstition.'[10]

3. Inculturation theology—the attempt to keep the best

If the Celtic revival represents an engagement of the Church with its own history, there are also those working more directly with native, pre-Christian spiritualities in an attempt to bring the best of them into a Christian framework—or to see the Christian faith incarnated in the native context. These theologians and worship practitioners are engaging directly with the post-imperial, post-Christian fascination with first peoples' cultures. The collapse of modernity has brought the opportunity to re-evaluate the Church's historic rejection of these cultures—not just their beliefs but their lifestyles, social structures, technologies and insights. If it has been possible for the Church to be incarnated for so long, and so deeply, in the modern 'story' of Western progress, then surely it can equally be incarnated into other, pre-modern cultures?

Michael Shirres, who died in 1997, was a Dominican priest who worked for twenty years among the Maori people indigenous to New Zealand. His life's work was to find points of connection between Maori culture, traditions and spirituality on the one hand and the Christian gospel on the other. He called this process inculturation:

Inculturation is a theological term which embraces two rich and seminal ideas, enculturation and incarnation. Enculturation involves growing into a culture which is a process which is continuous right through life. Incarnation is a theological term that expresses God's becoming a human being . . . In-culturation is a made-up word which signifies the process where Jesus, as a human, took on the culture of a particular people. Just as he became a Jew so he becomes a member of other communities, taking on their particular culture. As the Word was made flesh becoming a Jew, so "the Word is made flesh", becoming a member of each human family.[11]

Part of the process of inculturation, for Shirres, lay in the creation of prayers and liturgies which were thoroughly Christian and yet drew on the imagery, traditions and writings of the ancient Maori nation. This lifelong question took on new poignancy when, in 1994, Shirres was diagnosed with a form of Motor Neurone Disease and told that he was dying. Throughout his final years, at various stages of incapacity, he spoke of 'the experience of the love of Jesus' brought to him by the words of a Maori chant for the person dying:

'Your heart. My heart. You give me your dying heart. Let me give you my living heart. Cross over to life. Rise up above!'[12] By taking this prayer out of its pagan context and into his knowledge of Christ, Shirres found strength, encouragement and comfort.

The transitional generations have grown up with an inquisitive respect for pre-modern cultures—the stories that inspired us before the Western dream took centre stage and pushed them to the margins. For the many who struggle with issues of origin, ethnicity, roots and identity, the recovery of these stories and the worship of a non-white Jesus go together. For these generations, a Church which honours and embraces the very best in all cultures will be a Church worth knowing.

4. The post-Charismatics—to Pentecost and beyond

A fourth area in which young people are exploring the possibilities of adapting to a post-Christian context is among a new generation of Charismatics—young people who are embracing the emotional dimension of faith, making use very often of dance music and video technology and creating a worship experience built around the dynamic experience of the presence of God. Intuitive, creative, holistic, relational, these young people are rejecting the notion of the church as an institution and working instead through cells and small congregations, deeply committed to peer relationships and to an indwelt, '24/7'[13] spirituality. 'How can you get excited about God in an old-style church, sitting in a row of pews?' asks Russ Oliver, founder of the Interface events in southern England. 'At our events we shout if we feel angry and cry if we feel sad. It's more like a pop concert or a football match.'[14]

As well as prioritising the experience of faith, these groups are exploring new models of community; reclaiming a Christian commitment to social justice; celebrating the whole spectrum of the arts and creativity, and gleefully sending missionaries into the post-modern sub-cultures of dance clubs, skate parks, fashion houses and the music industry.

What these four strands or developments have in common, alongside their willingness to explore new ways of expressing the Christian faith in a post-modern culture, is a willingness, more crucially, to abandon some of the ways in which the faith has been expressed in modernity. Unless young people are allowed to take hold of faith for themselves—to test its durability; to explore its boundaries; to deconstruct and reconstruct its style; to reroot it in the soil of their own lives—they will neither embrace nor uphold Christianity in the cultures of the coming century. As long as the structures and styles of our faith are too precious and untouchable to be released into the hands of the young, we are doomed to a 'rapidly expiring shelf-life'.[15]

As the post-Christian era takes firm hold of our spirituality, more and more young people from the transitional generations will seek expressions of worship and entrypoints to faith which are new and different. As George Barna expresses it, 'As we introduce new approaches to ministry, many of the fundamental elements of the Church will undoubtedly be redefined.'[16]

Those more established in the existing expressions of church, who might find aspects of these new models by turns frightening, disturbing, exhilarating and bizarre, will need to make space for young people; to encourage and support experimentation; to offer support in both success and failure—in the words of Martin Scott, to 'bless the strange ways of God'[17] Studies in 'paradigm shifts', a concept developed by scientist Thomas Kuhn, reveal that 'Paradigm shifters are usually found at the edge, not the centre of the existing paradigm'.[18] What new expressions of the Christian faith are growing already on the fringes of the current Church, ready to offer spiritual experience, direction, fulfilment and purpose to the post-Christian generations? Whatever they are, they are our hope. 'The mystery of the gospel,' Leslie Newbiggin has said, 'is not entrusted to the Church to be buried in the ground. It is entrusted to the Church to be risked in the change and interchange of the spiritual commerce of humanity.'[19] The question we must ask is not 'dare we change', but 'dare we not'. 'We cannot be born anew,' Paul Tillich has written, 'if the power of the old is not broken within us.'[20]

Let those who find such a challenge too much even to think about, consider, by way of a parable, The Legend of the Unbreakable Teapot.

The precise origins of the unbreakable teapot were buried in time. It had come into the family when Great-Grandfather Joe, wandering the muddy trenches of Ypres at the height of the 1914–18 war, found it in a bombed-out farmhouse. Certain no one would return to claim it, he kept it for his own.

By the time Joe returned, war-weary, to marriage and industry in England, the teapot had become a legend. Through torrents of shelling and sniper fire; through trench manoeuvres and interminable route-marches across the burnt and scarred French fields; through nine months of warfare on an apocalyptic scale, Joe had carried his teapot, and his teapot had remained unbroken. Even its spout, that most fragile of teapot appendages, was intact.

'It's a miracle!' Joe's mates had declared.

'It's an omen,' Joe had answered, clinging to the hope of survival.

Somewhere along the way, and for ever after, the old china pot became known as 'the unbreakable teapot'. Back home, it was given pride of place on the kitchen shelves. It was a talking-point, an excuse to reminisce about the war. When Joe's kids came along, the teapot was the focus of a hundred stories to enthral them—stories they would later tell their own children. The darkness and horror, the friends won and lost and always the unbreakable teapot, surviving at the heart of it all like the miracle of life itself.

Until Joe passed it on to his eldest, Tom, the teapot was in daily use—earning its keep, providing for the family's needs. 'This is not to be an idle curiosity,' Joe told the family, 'It's a working pot—and as long as I drink tea it will be.'

Tom's eldest, Roger, grew up with the teapot on the shelf. Year by year, its legend grew, even as its usefulness diminished. New stories were added:

'It's been dropped, three times, on the concrete pantry floor,' they would say, 'and never a scratch to show for it.'

'It saved my grandad's life,' Roger would add, apocryphally. 'Blocked a bullet heading right for his heart.' Margaret, Roger's wife, took care to dust and clean the teapot once a week. She had been fond of Joe, and enjoyed the memory of him. But she had her own tastes in chinaware, and could easily afford a better quality. Besides, who could say when a kettle-full of boiling water might not finally crack the old pot? Better to keep it safe than risk its loss. Apart from the weekly dusting, the unbreakable teapot was rarely off the shelf.

The crisis came when young Joe, named after his great-grandfather, was just ten. Like his sisters and cousins, he had grown up knowing all about the teapot. Rarely had he been in the company of Grandfather Tom without the stories being told—Tom conjuring up, through the magic of words, the very presence of his long-dead father as he sat, turning the teapot in his hand, speaking with reverence and awe of what it meant to him, and how nothing—not war, nor water, nor a drop on the floor—could break it. Young Joe, whose own hands had never touched the precious pot, would listen wide-eyed.

'Why not?' he would ask his mother, when she told him for the millionth time that the pot was out of bounds to him on its high shelf, that he was never, not ever, to touch it.

'Because it's precious,' she would say with genuine awe.

'It's been in our family for three generations already, and one day it will be yours—but it's not for a child to touch.'

Sometimes, when he was alone in the kitchen, Joe would look up to the high shelf, stretched like a skyscraper above him. He would examine the cold hardness of the pantry floor, kicking his toes against it until it hurt, and wonder at the things he had been told. And much as he loved Grandfather Tom, and the stories of Great Grandfather Joe; and much as he trusted his parents, and believed what they told him; and much as he wanted the stories to be true, he couldn't help wondering if after all, in the real world, they were not.

It was Grandfather Tom's seventy-fifth birthday. Relatives had come out of the woodwork to gather at Joe's house to celebrate. Grandfather Tom, happy at the heart of it all, spent much of the afternoon with assorted combinations of grandchildren on his knee or at his feet, repeating once more the legends of the unbreakable teapot; conjuring up, again, the presence of old Joe.

Young Joe, meanwhile, was shocked by the irreverence of his own thoughts.

'If it's unbreakable, why can't I touch it?' he asked himself in silence. 'If the stories are true, why keep it on the shelf?'

The relatives were gathered on the front drive, making their farewells and extracting cars from the sardine-parking. Grandfather Tom, in his wheelchair, was positioned to the left of the front porch, in the shadow of a Rhododendron bush, from where he could watch them all leave. Roger and Margaret were at either side of the front gate to pipe their guests ashore. It was Joe's Aunt Peggy—Roger's sister—who noticed first.

'What the . . . ?!' she cried, as her arm shot upwards to point out the horror, and every eye followed its line. Four generations gasped and held their breath.

At the very top of the house, where the dormer window of the attic bedroom reached almost to the edge of the roof, young Joe was leaning out. One foot set on the window ledge, he held with one hand to the frame—his body swinging out over the drive. In his free hand, its spout to the wind, he held the unbreakable teapot.

From opposite sides of the drive, Roger and Margaret realised at the same moment what it was that their son was about to do. The screamed words left their mouths in unrehearsed unison, 'No, Joe, don't . . ..'

Too late. Their heads held in horror, the assembled relatives saw the teapot slip from young Joe's hand, to begin its graceful fall to the ground. Every faced was contorted with horror. Except that of Grandfather Tom. Alone in his chair, he looked up at Joe. He could see the concentration on the boy's face. He could see the pot, falling like a stone towards the tarmac. And as he saw it, he thought of old Joe, his father. And smiled.

Notes

1 Pete Greig, 'E Generation', *Compass Magazine*, spring 1998. Adapted from the forthcoming book *The Awakening Cry.*

2 Loren Mead in the foreword to Robert N. Nash, *An 8-Track Church in a CD World* (Smyth and Helwys, 1998). Details at http://www.helwys.com/8track.html

3 Karl Marx, 1835, quoted in *Bread for the Journey*, Issue 2 1998 (CWR: Farnham).

4 Loren Mead, *The Once and Future Church* (The Alban Institute: Bethesda, Md, 1991).

5 George Barna, *The Second Coming of.*

6 Oscar Romero, 'The Last Homily', 24 March 1980, reproduced in *Romero, Martyr for Liberation* (Catholic Institute for International Relations: London, 1982).

7   For links to alternative worship groups, visit http://www.greenbelt.org.uk/altgrps/

8   Esther De Waal, *The Celtic Way of Prayer*, (Hodder and Stoughton: London 1996), introduction.

9   Ian Bradley, *The Celtic Way* (Darton, Longman and Todd: London 1993), p. 74.

10   Michael Mitton, *Restoring the Woven Cord : Strands of Celtic Christianity for the Church Today*, (Darton, Longman and Todd: London, 1995).

11   Michael Shirres, 'Inculturation', Internet article at http://www.homepages.ihug.co.nz/~dominic/intro.html

12   Michael Shirres, 'My Life', Internet article at http://www.homepages.ihug.co.nz/~dominic/mylife.html

13   See p. 66.

14   Russ Oliver, quoted in Helen Chappell, 'It's hip to be holy', *New Statesman and Society*, 8 September 1995.

15   George Barna, *op. cit.*, 1998, p. 1.

16   *Ibid.*

17   Martin Scott, *Pioneer People*, private conversation.

18   Leadership Network, 'When the Horse is Dead, Dismount', Internet article at http://www.leadnet.org/d1dnetfax11.html

19   Leslie Newbiggin, *The Open Secret* (SPCK: London 1995), p. 189.

20   Paul Tillich, *The Shaking of the Foundations* (SCM Press, 1949).

PART THREE

Root Growth
Resources for the Management of Change

14

PILLAR TO POST

If you are among those who are experiencing a ride on the wild side, if you are feeling out of control, let me whisper an important word in your ear. All appearances to the contrary, the Creator God is quietly transforming our "future shocked" world. While we may feel out of control, our God isn't.

Tom Sine[1]

Get up and eat, for the journey is too much for you.

The angel of God, to Elijah[2]

Taking an overview of the 'five posts of generation X and beyond', it is not hard to see why some in the Christian faith community feel threatened by these waves of social change. These are not peripheral areas of faith and practice under-going minor alterations, these are core areas, for some the very pillars of the faith, deconstructing and reforming. Both literally and figuratively, we are being driven from pil-lar to post. Even a cursory glance at the kinds of questions our journey through the culture junction has raised will reveal the breadth and depth of these changes—questions of the nature and structure of the Church, and of what it means to belong; of the place and treatment of the Bible in non-book culture; of the place of evangelism and conversion in pick-and-mix times; of the future of mission on a changing planet; of the style and content of Christian worship. It is hardly surprising that for many, especially those who have invested most heavily in the existing models and structures, change is a demanding and difficult journey.

The regeneration gap

This chapter suggests six steps in the management of personal and corporate change which might contribute to an easier ride, and give confidence to those just setting out. The six do not function in any set order, and are not set out as any kind of programme. Rather, they are six suggestions to explore, six doorways into change. They are intended to help those faced with change to make a real and considered impact on the future we all face.

Impact 1—Investigate social change

> It is not that those deep things of the faith have changed. Rather, the structures in which we have housed them and the thought-forms with which we explained them have grown archaic. New languages and new structures will be needed for the gospel truth to be articulated in this world of postmodernity.[3]

One of the great enemies of constructive change is apathy—we don't change because we are simply not interested in changing. We have our own small world well ordered and complete—what goes on outside the windows is of little value to us. If this book has achieved anything, I hope it has proved the inadequacy of such an attitude and, for some, burst the bubble of virtual reality. The world is changing, and the changes it brings can be merciless. Our engagement with change begins with the simple act of being interested. For some, this will mean exploring areas they have previously chosen to ignore—changes in technology, or philosophy, or popular spirituality; for others it will mean listening afresh to those immersed in change, not least the younger generations. Only if we will begin with investigating, exploring, examining, gathering data—with throwing the net wide and letting the catch inform us—will we be able to negotiate and manage the changes demanded of us. Five key suggestions for achieving impact 1 are:

- Buy (or better still subscribe to) a magazine covering an area about which you know little but which is on the leading edge of change—computer technology, club and dance, youth culture, management, commerce. Read it with one question foremost in your thinking, 'What does this tell me the future might be like?' Cut and keep helpful articles on key areas, then add others from newspapers, other magazines and the Internet.
- Identify individuals who have recently made big changes in their lives: those who have moved from employment to self-employment, those adopting a new faith, those working in new industries, those returning to study after a long period in work. Ask them how and why they made the changes they have made. Ask yourself how much of their experience relates to wider cultural changes.
- Get on to the Internet. Search and surf, using key words and site tip-offs. Join a future-focussed chat group, or create your own with half a dozen friends or colleagues on e-mail. If computers frighten the life out of you, sign up for a user-friendly course at a local college.

- Talk to people younger than yourself, especially those whose lifestyles most challenge you. Ask them why they live as they do, not so that you can judge but so that you can know. Start with those known to you before you graduate to strangers!

- Look into a field parallel to your own, but with a different emphasis. Protestants, for instance, have much to learn from the ways in which the Catholic Church deals with change, and vice versa. Business leaders and the voluntary sector can learn from one another. Christian charities can learn from the experience of those of a different faith confession or none. Many of the changes we are facing only come into focus when you can see the big picture—like the Earth viewed from space. Often this will emerge only through inter-disciplinary thinking.

Impact 2—Make space for personal change

Not only does he bring about change, but in a significant sense God himself experiences change. After God acts, the universe is different and God's experience of the universe is different.[4]

A second great enemy of change is over-commitment. The over-committed are often pursuing the most noble and high-minded of motivations, but they are so tied up in maintaining the status quo that they haven't the time nor the energy even to contemplate change, let alone deliver it. Business and career, church and faith, family and home— all are capable of submerging us in such a weight of important tasks that we forget what made them important in the first place. But none of us is so well established, so fully formed, that we can afford to dismiss personal change. Few will have the luxury of calling, 'Halt!' to everything, but most can call halt to something and create space on the margins in which new ideas can form. The irony of over-commitment is that it is often focussed on the very structures and programmes that need to change. We have spent so long cultivating our personal portfolio of causes, committees and conflicts that it is unthinkable to abandon unfinished tasks and battles—even though the significance of victory would fade if only we allowed new paradigms to emerge. To change direction requires more space and time than to go on without changing. Here are five suggestions for achieving Impact 2:

- Set future-focussed core goals, values and purposes for your life—whether in terms of career, family, leisure or faith. Take time to make sure these goals are genuine and balanced, then look for activities you are engaged in which do not contribute to their fulfilment. Begin to plan your withdrawal from these activities.
- Commit one regular slice of your time—an evening each week, a morning once a month, two full days a year—to focussing on new areas of thinking, learning, exploration and prayer. This might be through additional reading, a short course or a prayer retreat alone or with others. Whatever it is, the key is that it should be focussed on listening and learning rather than on activity, and that the commitment, once made, should be kept. Even if all you can redeem is one hour each week, redeem it, and use it as space for change.
- Rediscover walking, whether it is in the open countryside at weekends or in the town centre during a lunchbreak. Re-embrace the slower pace of the pedestrian and open your eyes to what is around you. Use regular walking time to observe, reflect, think and pray.
- Invest in relationships—as a couple, as parents and children, as colleagues and friends, as strangers on a bus.

Reinvent the lost art of conversation. Learn to ask open questions, and to listen to replies. Recover a passionate interest in people—in their motivations, their struggles, their hopes and dreams. The questions in your own life that never get answered are the ones you never ask. Where the relationship is secure, be ready to be vulnerable about your own struggles—you are more likely than not to find them common.

- Think seriously about potential 'big changes'. Job, location, income, lifestyle, timestyle, friendships, leisure patterns, possessions, ambitions: these are the building-brick decisions from which our lives are constructed. They do not change easily and, as a general rule, the longer it is since the choice was made, the harder it is to change it. But it may be that time taken to reflect, pray and invest in relationships will highlight a need for change on such a scale. Sometimes it is only when we stop that we see how far off-course we are.

Impact 3—Prioritise the young

> We will tell the next generation the praiseworthy deeds of the Lord, his power and the wonders he has done.[5]

That the future belongs to those who are presently young is the truism to end all truisms. Strange, then, that so little of our thinking reflects this. When we think about the future, we often fall into the trap of projecting our own experience forward and of assuming that the concerns of our own day and generation will remain the concerns of tomorrow. The reality couldn't be more different, and it is essential that our focus shift to those who will both shape and inherit tomorrow—the 'next' generations. In Psalm 78, this includes two generations—our children and our children's children.[6] If our thinking is to focus genuinely on these generations (for our purposes these fall somewhere within Generation X, the Millennials and whatever comes next), then so must other considerations. We will not achieve Impact 3 without re-evaluating:

- Our budgets. How much of the money we allocate in churches, communities and projects actually meets the needs and aspirations of the rising generations? Do our financial decisions genuinely reflect the disproportionate stake they have in the future?
- Our strategies. How many of our strategic decisions (think of planning, buildings, activities, events, training, purchases, literature, decor, facilities) are targeted towards these needs? How many of our decisions would be different if we said at every stage, the future is youth and youth are the future? When was the last time we asked them? About anything?
- Our use of time. Might it be possible to audit our own timestyle—in terms of thinking time, activity time, study time, work time, etc., and ask how much of it deals with the needs of the rising generations? Even if we are employed in an old people's home, might we make a 5% time-investment in the future?
- Our trust. When was the last time we took the risk of trusting a younger person with a task we might otherwise place in 'safe hands'? In the case of the Church, it is the safe hands that have strangled us—why not give the risky hands a try?

Impact 4—Accept what you find

The crucial issue for Christians is the extent to which we are prepared to accept the integrity of those adopting a different approach from ours. If we insist that any approach other than ours signifies lack of integrity and lack of true faith, fragmentation of the body of Christ is inevitable.[7]

A significant block to creative change is the rush to form premature judgements: literally, prejudices. Before our brains can fully assess the implications of a new idea, our mouths have already formed the words 'It'll never work.' This is a particular problem for those in the Christian faith community, who have become so adept at defending the truth from error that they stop every new suggestion at the door and body-search it. Pouring the cold water of judgement on every creative idea, we stunt growth, inhibit exploration and, by implication, block change. In a time of transition this is death. When a community has lost its source of food, it is not wise to lynch every hunter who suggests where new food might be found. Transition demands that we allow the new to emerge and show itself, and that we allow the young the freedom to explore. This is not to suggest that we abandon all judgement and embrace the new for its own sake. It may be necessary to keep a critical and analytical faculty loaded and ready to use—but it may serve us well to take our finger off the trigger. When we are faced with the new, the extreme, the bizarre, the challenging, our first thought should not be 'Burn the heretic!' but 'Hold your fire!' Who knows when what seems at first bizarre might not prove, at closer quarters, to be your salvation. Author Gareth Jones, in exploring the very specific field of controversy in the Church, has suggested five questions as the basis for a group discussion.[8] All five, and the suggestion that you discuss them with your peers, will help significantly towards achieving Impact 4:

1. What do you consider as central and peripheral issues for Christians? How do you distinguish between the two?
2. To what extent do you think evangelical Christians have freedom to explore new areas of thought or practice? Give examples of what you think might or might not be acceptable.
3. What measures do you think should be taken to avoid confrontation within churches?
4. 'Compromise' is often regarded as a dirty word, since it stands for accepting second-best. Do you agree with this, or is it sometimes the path to be followed by Christians? Try and think of specific examples.
5. If you are faced with a novel way of doing something, how do you react? Discuss the various reactions within the group. Think of ways we can build on these initial reactions and make them more Christian.

Impact 5—Champion hinge leaders

The mainline denominations are bleeding. Their churches have more pew than flock, and unless they change, they have more history than future.

Charles Trueheart[9]

One of the reasons many people find it hard to embrace change is that they genuinely and honestly don't understand what is happening. We struggle, as Loren Mead has written, 'to make sense out of the changes that seem to sweep over our culture and threaten to make many things we do obsolete'.[10] We know how to construct good decisions from good understanding—but we don't have it, and we don't know where to get it. Such is the speed of change that everything about the challenge we face—the people involved, their language codes, their identity and aspirations—are alien to us. We are from Venus, they are from Mars. It is for this reason that we stand urgently in need of a generation of Hinge Leaders—people sufficiently at home in the new to understand it, and sufficiently at home in the old to help us understand it.

Hinge leaders have attachments in both cultures—in our current situation they are drawn for the most part from GenX—and they have the capacity to hold in tension the best of both old and new, and to broker communication across the culture gap. Churches, communities, businesses, families, nations can all benefit from the go-between services of hinge leaders. Theirs is the voice that will open up the future for us, and theirs is the vision that will first bring the new into the old. But they are not without need of support for themselves. Living in two worlds is a tough call, and you are as likely to be rejected by both as accepted by either. Here are six steps you can take to achieve Impact 5 by nurturing, supporting and championing hinge leaders:

- Find out who they are. Who are the GenX leaders on the fringe of existing communities and structures who have an intuitive grasp on the future? Chances are, they will be found among those who struggle with existing paradigms and don't fit easily into existing plans.
- Give them time and attention. Let them know that you are there to support them. Ask them what their needs are. Provide friendship, training, resources, inspiration. Become allies in bringing the future to birth.
- Listen to their vision. Ask them what the priorities should be; what changes they are looking for and why; what they see and hear from their stand-point on the margins. Trust them to tell you where your own direction could change.
- Find room for them in the structures. This might be on the fringe of things, in a quiet corner—but it must be

room in which they are empowered to pursue their vision. Putting hinge leaders onto committees to give the appearance of sharing power is pointless and unjust; find them a space, no matter how small, where they have real power.

- Get behind them. Emotionally, financially, structurally. Become known for your support of them. Defend their record, tell their story, validate their experiments. Put your trust of them into action. Share with them the joys and pains of success and failure. Coach them, encourage them, resource them.

- Stay close to them. A relationship of accountability has to be just that—a relationship. You are not a champion of innovation in which you have no stake or involvement and of which you have no understanding. Risk allows for the possibility both of triumph and of disaster, and your presence will be needed to manage either.

Impact 6—Take the plunge!

Change is the angel of a changeless God[11]

Imagine yourself climbing the steps to a high diving-board. Proud of your courage, you ascend to the highest platform. You share with fellow-divers the joy of being numbered among the brave. You step forward to the very edge of the board, which trembles under you. You have mentally rehearsed the move a thousand times; you have overcome all the early anxieties and exaggerated fears. But there is one final barrier—a new and unimagined terror that doesn't grip you until your toes are wrapped over the very end of the board, and the pool below appears as a tiny patch of water in the far distance. You haven't yet won the battle— you have to jump.

Dramatic imagery for some, but for others an accurate picture. It's all very well to investigate change; to make time and space for it; to think 'the future is youth and youth are the future'. It's all very well to suspend your judgement of others, even to identify and champion change-leaders. But there comes a time when it is right to make real changes for yourself, and it is costly. To be aware of change, to broadly welcome it is one thing; to cut right into core activities and make significant changes is another. It can cost in terms of power relinquished, ambitions abandoned, support sacrificed. It can mean surrendering competence, becoming a novice again. It can mean relinquishing known success to embrace the possibility of failure. The new, by definition, begins smaller than the old, and runs the risk of infant death. But the new, very often, is where God is. As you consider Impact 6, ask yourself:

- Is there a key area in which you could soon 'take the plunge' and change your life?
- What is there in your current work, home or lifestyle that you love very much, but might well have to abandon as you embrace change? What does the diving-board represent for you?
- As you have examined the 'five posts' analysis, what areas have been highlighted for you as personal hot-zones?
- How does your imagined 'Church of the tomorrow' differ from your experience of the 'Church of today'? What steps lead from one to the other? What is the first of these steps?
- Who do you most admire for their capacity to embrace and manage change? What would it take for you to emulate them?
- What new dreams and visions have surfaced in you as

you have considered the challenge of change in this chapter?

- If all of your current commitments were miraculously cancelled as of tomorrow, what would you spend the next five years doing?
- What three things could you do within the next five days to implement one of the six Impacts given here? (Buy a book or magazine; talk to a specific individual; arrange a discussion evening; research a given theme on the web, etc.)

Retrenchment or rebirth?

The great drama teacher Konstantin Stanislavsky would occasionally insist that his students, before being allowed to leave the room, should say 'Goodnight' to him in fifty different tones of voice.[12] His point was that creativity—the capacity to think beyond the box; to explore new avenues; to be original; to find diversity, variety and freshness in the everyday—must be worked at and fought for. It is easier to say goodnight the way we've always said it than it is to find fifty new ways, but the actor who takes the easy option will achieve all but nothing. In the event, Stanislavsky shaped and inspired some of the greatest actors of stage and screen in our century, and his legacy holds power to this day. Creativity takes work; new thinking can be exhausting, even painful—but without it we are doomed to stay within existing paradigms, saying goodnight for ever in the same dull voice and losing contact, bit by bit, with our audience. New birth is messy, bloody, painful, disruptive, difficult, demanding, inconvenient. But without new birth, all we're doing is dying. To use Mike Riddel's chilling words: 'I think this is the call of God to the Western Church at the end of the second millennium: to change or to die.'[13]

Notes

1   Tom Sine, *Mustard Seed versus McWorld* (Monarch: Crowborough, 1999), introduction.

2   I Kings 19:7.

3   Loren Mead in the foreword to Robert N. Nash, *An 8-Track Church in a CD World* (Smyth and Helwys, 1998). http://www.helwys.com/8trackmead.html

4   Richard Rice in Pinnock et al, *The Openness of God: A biblical Challenge to the Traditional Understanding of God* (IVP/Paternoster, 1994), p. 36.

5   Psalm 78:4.

6   Psalm 78:6.

7   Gareth Jones, *Coping With Controversy* (Solway: Carlisle, 1996), p. 42.

8   *Ibid.*, p. 45.

9   Charles Trueheart, 'Welcome to the Next Church', *Atlantic Monthly*, August 1996.

10   Loren Mead, *op. cit.*

11   Archbishop William Temple, quoted in Cray et al, *The Post Evangelical Debate* (Triangle: London, 1997), p. 74.

12   Cited in Colin Morris, *God-in-a-Box* (Hodder and Stoughton: London, 1984).

13   Mike Riddell, *Threshold of the Future* (SPCK: London, 1998).

15

TSAR WARS
New Models of Leadership

Good leaders grow people, bad leaders stunt them; good leaders serve their followers, bad leaders enslave them.

Sir Adrian Cadbury[1]

Go to the people. Live among them. Start with what they have. Build on what they know. And when the deed is done, the mission accomplished, of the best leaders the people will say, "We have done it ourselves."

Loa Tzu[2]

In his exploration of the Holy Island of Lindisfarne,[3] Magnus Magnusson describes some of the cultural distinctions between the Celtic and Roman approaches to the Christian faith.

Celtic monks lived in conspicuous poverty; Roman monks lived well . . . Celtic bishops practised humility, Roman bishops paraded pomp. Celtic bishops were ministers of their flocks, Roman bishops were monarchs of their dioceses. Celtic clergymen said "Do as I do," and hoped to be followed; Roman clergymen said, "Do as I say," and expected to be obeyed.[4]

In citing these examples, Magnusson is touching on one of the key reasons for the renewed interest in all things Celtic, and one of the core arenas in which our culture is in crisis—the arena of leadership. Shaped by the uncertainties of postmodernity, and schooled in its ambivalence towards authority, the emerging generations are seeking out models of leadership far removed from the control and command approach characteristic of the twentieth century.

Remote controllers

Of all the charges laid at the door of the Church by many disaffected young people who in recent years have made the choice to leave, the most frequent and damning is the charge of controlling leadership. Styles of leadership forged in the certainties of modernity, fitted to the assembly-line routines of industrialism and built on the linear and literate thought-processes of print technology, are increasingly alien to a generation in search of new models. Generation X, according to Kevin Ford, have been 'burned by pathological models of authority'.[5] In the home and workplace, in communities and organisations, the massive changes shaking the foundations of our culture are calling for a new understanding and practice of the skills of leadership. For too many young people, there has been no distinction made between leading and controlling—to accept leadership and authority has been to accept control. Stifling creativity, stunting innovation and imagination, forcing uniformity, silencing dissent—controlling leadership acts like a blanket thrown over a crowd, subjugating the needs of the many who follow to the needs of the few who lead.

The claustrophobia this produces is pushing many people to seek fresh air and freedom outside the confines of the Church—not because they hate the gospel, but because they hate the bondage that the gospel has been made to bring. As Meic Pearse of London Bible College asks,

> Are we equipping the saints or fostering their dependency on us? Can we let go of our scarcely admitted itch to control or bolster our positions? Pastors and preachers, housegroup leaders, Sunday school teachers, worship leaders, youth workers: we all want our egos fed. It's time to start asking, "Who's feeding whom?"[6]

Whatever else the current wave of social change calls for, it calls for a reformation in the Church's understanding of leadership.

Resourceful friends

Sociologist Bob Holman[7] developed the concept of 'resourceful friends' in the context of community development, essentially to describe the ways in which ordinary people can help each other in communities in which hierarchical structures of authority have broken down or lost their impact.[8] He did not intend the term as a definition of leadership, but it does provide an excellent summary of the kind of leaders the new century will demand—leaders who come alongside; who seek to encourage and resource; who see their best success as investing in the success of others. This is not to imply that such leaders do not exist already, nor that these 'soft' skills are not present in many contemporary leaders: only that these have not been the primary skills called for in the twentieth century. As our culture shifts, it will call for a different emphasis, a different balance of gift and skill.

Jim Partridge is a young leader in his twenties who has observed leadership at close hand in a range of church and para-church organisations. Professionally, he is a middle-manager for a major Christian organisation, with a brief which includes the oversight of an 'emerging leaders' process. He has also recently joined the leadership team of his own local church. Like many younger and emerging leaders, he is convinced that the new situation into which we are moving will require new models of effective leadership, and a new attitude in those who exercise it. Surveying the current church scene, he has identified four key demands which the twenty-first century will place on its leaders:

- A willingness to listen and change;
- A willingness to take risks and move forward;
- A willingness to serve and obey;
- A willingness to trust and delegate;[9]

Together, these four will form a matrix of priorities for those exercising leadership in church and society: the essential leader's checklist for the early decades of millennium three.

1. Check that you're looking, listening and learning

Leadership was once about hard skills such as planning, finance and business analysis. When command and control ruled the corporate world, the leaders were heroic rationalists who moved people around like pawns and fought like stags . . . Now, if the gurus and experts are right, leadership is increasingly concerned with soft skills—teamwork, communication and motivation.[10]

The shift in industry from 'hard' to 'soft' skills is now well documented. At its heart is the drive for co-operation, for leadership built on negotiation, motivation and mutual benefit rather than coercion, control and fear. When the Industrial Society[11] surveyed three thousand people from businesses across the UK to determine what they saw as the best and worst traits of leaders, the five weakest areas of less successful leaders were cited as:

- they fail to be sensitive to people's feelings;
- they fail to recognise other people's stress;
- they fail to develop and guide their staff;
- they fail to encourage feedback on their own performance;
- they fail to consult those affected before making decisions.[12]

Parallel research has not been carried out among those attending (or leaving) churches: but can we really believe that if it were it would not produce very similar results?

Beyond the immediate 'soft' skills of listening for the sake of co-operation and motivation, twenty-first century leaders will also be called upon to look, listen and learn for their own survival in a changing environment. In a static culture it is enough to learn skills once, perhaps in college, and to dedicate a life to practising them. In a culture reinventing itself every five to seven years this is untenable. 'A new paradigm means that everyone goes back to zero.', advises the Leadership Network, 'You lose any leverage you had in the old paradigm. Anticipatory, not reactive leadership is required.'[13] To be a leader in the coming decades will mean, by definition, to be a lifelong learner—not only gaining new skills, but being able to adapt existing skills to new situations with dramatic frequency: with one eye on the task in hand and one eye on the horizon. '*We need to become experts at reading and understanding cultural maps*' author David Fisher has advised.[14]

The shifting sands of our cultural environment are not only the context in which we must work, they are also our most potent source of up-to-the-minute learning. Twenty-first century leaders will find themselves asking constantly, 'What have I learned today ... this week ... this year?' Those unable to listen, and to learn, will soon find that they are unable to lead.

2. Check out your imagination, inspiration and innovation

> Christ came as a liberator. Christ understood that we as humans were for ever held to the ground by the pull of gravity—our ordinariness, our mediocrity—and it was through his example that he gave our imaginations the freedom to rise and fly.[15]

Leadership that doesn't inspire the imaginations of those who choose to follow is little more than cleverly disguised bureaucracy. 'The greatest leaders are those who explain the world,' Tony Benn writes, 'and thus help us to gain control of our destiny.'[16] If human beings did not need help in understanding their times and inspiration to overcome fear and inertia, they would not need leaders. It is crucial that leaders see this and take seriously their responsibility to inspire—to switch on the imaginative functions of those they lead. This is just the opposite of closing down creativity because it is too much of a threat.

The capacity to inspire courage, to give vision against the odds, to create dreams out of the raw materials of fear and uncertainty is more needed than ever in a context of fluidity and change.

> Leading people (as opposed to simply managing them) in a new direction means reshaping their view of the world. It means shattering their sense of stability, tossing out their old

standards of success, and prying them loose from the status quo. And then it means replacing what you've wiped out with a new, coherent and energising vision of what you believe the future can and should be.[17]

Every institution in our culture, not least its churches, is crying out for the kinds of leaders who will take risks and foster innovation, finding new solutions to old problems and meeting new problems head on. 'One quality you can't learn, but which is present in a great leader,' says politician Paddy Ashdown, 'is courage. Not physical courage, though that can be important, but moral courage. All other skills vanish like the morning dew if you haven't got courage.'[18] The 'soft' skills of looking, listening and learning demand that leaders should include and consult, treating people as people not pawns—but this does not absolve them of the responsibility to cast vision. In an era of unprecedented change, our culture of confusion and contradiction is crying out for vision-casters.

3. Check up on your servanthood, sacrifice and self-giving

The best kind of leaders serve the people they are leading. A servant leader needs to know what people need in order to help them to lead themselves. Jesus Christ was a prime example—it is all about empowering, not dominating.[19]

Over the generations, many different symbols have come to represent the power and role of leadership: the five stars on a general's uniform; the huge executive office and chauffeured limousine; the bishop's mitre; the two short words 'Right Hon.'. Yet the only symbol that could be said to capture the essence of Christian leadership is one which rarely arises: that of the towel. Jesus' act of foot-washing is the fountain from which the resources of Christian leadership arise and flow. There is no New Testament model of leadership which is not servanthood.

As the new generations struggle to come to terms with their own brokenness; their disillusionment with authority; the dysfunctionality of their home experience, they stand more than ever in need of the kind of leaders more attuned to washing feet than making speeches. '*To build something enduring,*' writes George Bullard, '*you have to think beyond yourself. To help your congregation succeed fifty years from now, you have to have a servant-leadership mentality that focuses on the congregation succeeding, not just yourself.*'[20] This may well be the greatest contribution that the Church can make to the whole arena of leadership development, that it has a framework which makes sense of the very acts of service and love the culture is looking for. The mysterious balance of power and powerlessness evident in the life of Jesus, his capacity to be single-minded yet open, to move resolutely forwards in the pursuit of his destiny and yet not violate the destiny of others, to hold to non-violence and yet be strong, even strident, when needed—in short to serve and yet lead—these are the very qualities twenty-first century leadership calls for.

4. Check if you're trusting in talent and team

It may sound like a paradox, but good leaders, too, are willing to be led. They must trust those they appoint, and then allow them to get on with the job.'[21]

It is ironic that some of the leaders who ask most insistently that those who follow should trust their vision without questions, struggle themselves to trust those around them.

But trust is a leadership commodity increasing in value by the day. Leaders who are unwilling to trust those they lead will never see them break out of low-skill patterns of dependency: growth comes through being given something to achieve. Some of the ways in which leaders can demonstrate trust, and mobilise the talents of their team are:

- By recruiting team members more talented than themselves.
- By practising 'give and let go'—give the responsibility, let go of the strings that tie it to you.
- By seeing every task as a team task.
- By delegating 50% more tasks than you feel comfortable delegating.
- By giving team members 20% more responsibility than they feel comfortable carrying.
- By being 100% committed to the success of others, and only 75% committed to your own.

If these four challenges offer a framework within which to re-evaluate the approach to leadership in the light of a culture in transition, there are two further attributes essential to the effective leader: an embracing of gender-balance and a focus on the future.

The tender gender

> God was not the issue. I still believe in him. But the church was all about the power of a few men. It's a man's church and some of the ways that women and young girls are treated are disgusting.[22]

For many observers of the current scene, the changes demanded by our shifting culture add up to the leadership equivalent of gender re-assignment—with the primarily male skills of command and control being replaced by the gentler, female skills of encouragement and nurture. Sarah, an ex-member of a UK church with a particularly strident view of male leadership, shows us just how important such a transformation can be. Many both within and outside the Christian community see this as the one key issue. James Robertson, in his influential *The Sane Alternative,* goes so far as to characterise the whole transition through which our culture is moving as a shift from the HE (hyper-expansionist) to the SHE (sane, humane, ecological) future.[23] According to Susan Cuff, CEO of recruitment consultancy Best International, women are better than men at today's style of leadership because '*women tend to create harmony, and we see situations in the round and not straight up and down*'.[24] Amin Rajan, CEO of CREATE, the Centre for Research in Employment and Technology in Europe, supports this view. '*It is a gender issue,*' he says '*Women cope better. They have empathy and good listening skills, even if they are outwardly aggressive.*'[25] Whatever your take on gender and leadership, there can be no doubt that many of the attributes of controlling leadership have been, over the centuries, predominantly male characteristics, and that the 'resourceful friends' model has a more feminine ethos. If the twenty-first century is to have the leaders it is crying out for, then it is clear that more of them must be women, and that those that are not must adopt a more gender-balanced approach. This is an insight recognised, and welcomed, by many in the rising generations, with a growing commitment to see a more balanced view of leadership, both in terms of the skills employed and of the gender of those employing them. If roughly half the population of the world is female, why aren't half its leaders?

A future not our own

Living in the great turbulence of El Salvador of the 1970s, Archbishop Oscar Romero was a man who knew what it was to witness sweeping social change—and to undergo dramatic personal change. His 'conversion to the poor' is one of the most celebrated Christian transformations since that of the Apostle Paul. He was a leader of quite astounding personal courage, who ultimately paid with his life for his determination to speak the truth on behalf of his people. In a sermon given to a group of priests in his care, he touches on the very essence of effective leadership.

> It helps, now and then, to step back and take the long view. The Kingdom is not only beyond our efforts, it is even beyond our vision. We accomplish in our lifetime only a tiny fraction of the magnificent enterprise that is God's work. Nothing we do is complete, which is another way of saying that the Kingdom always lies beyond us. No statement says all that can be said . . . No set of goals and objectives accomplishes the Church's mission. This is what we are about. We plant seeds that one day will grow. We water seeds already planted, knowing that they hold future promise. We lay foundations that will need further development. We provide yeast that produces effects far beyond our capabilities. We cannot do everything, and there is a sense of liberation in realising that. This enables us to do something, and to do it very well. It may not be complete, but it is a beginning, a step along the way, an opportunity for the Lord's grace to enter and do the rest. We may never see the end results, but that is the difference between the master builder and the worker. We are workers, not master builders; ministers not messiahs. We are prophets of a future not our own.[26]

If leadership is not about a focus on the future, what is it about? In a culture in transition, leaders are by definition those who see the future first—and those who are prepared to work for deferred rewards. Regardless of gender, age and social background, our culture is crying out for leaders who are ready to look ahead, to grasp intuitively the outlines of an emerging landscape and to chart a course that they and those who travel with them can follow. To chart such a course will mean, very often, to miss out on the rewards of staying put. There will be many in leadership who are just not ready for a frontier-town culture; who have invested too heavily in the acquired status of a settled life. These are leaders of whom Loren Mead says, 'Our difficulty in responding to the need to change comes from our love of the familiar and our desire to protect valued practices and structures from the past.'[27] But there will be others, some thrown into leadership for the first time, who thrive on the gold-rush mentality of social change, and bring a flood of new thinking to their responsibilities. These are the leaders who will break the cultural ice and blaze a trail into the future. Given the choice, which leaders would you follow?

If this book has been nothing else, it has been a call for those of the Christian faith community to be willing to focus on a future not our own: to invest our emotions, our intellect, our strength and our resources in the lives of the rising generations. They and only they have the right and responsibility to bring to birth a Church for the twenty-first century. They do so in the sure knowledge that the God they worship is out there, already, walking the planet; tasting its cultures; swimming in its streams. Our strategy must not be for survival but for rebirth. Not the Church we know today protected into its old age, but a new Church born in the fields of tomorrow—a Church that springs up from the ground on which, unknowing, we have thrown seeds. The Church of the future will arise not where the pillars of our certainties are grounded, but where the seeds of an ancient gospel reroot.

Notes

1 Sir Adrian Cadbury, quoted by Des Dearlove in 'First learn to be a follower,' *The Times*, London, 9 February 1999.

2 Lao Tzu, quoted by Tony Benn in 'Leadership into the 21st Century,' *The Times*, London, in Association with the Industrial Society, 9 February 1999.

3 For Lindisfarne information, see http://www.lindisfarne.org. uk/ index.htm

4 Magnus Magnusson, *Lindisfarne, the Cradle Island* (Oriel Press, 1984), p.58, quoted in Michael Mitton, *Restoring the Woven Cord* (Darton, Longman and Todd, London, 1995), p.15.

5 Kevin Ford *Jesus for a New Generation* (Hodder and Stoughton: London, 1996).

6 Meic Pearse, *Who's Feeding Whom*? (Solway: Carlisle, 1996), introduction.

7 See http://www.lion-publishing.co.uk/authors/meet_bob_ holman.htm

8 Bob Holman.

9 Jim Partridge, Spring Harvest, unpublished paper.

10 Stuart Crainer, 'The era of the hard man is over,' *The Times*, London, 9 February 1999.

11 http://www.indsoc.co.uk

12 Research published in February 1999 as 'Liberating Leadership 1999,' reported in *The Times*, London, 9 February 1999.

13 Leadership Network, 'When the Horse is Dead, Dismount', Internet article, 23 January 1997, http://www.leadnet.org/ d1dnetfax11.html

14 David Fisher, *The 21st Century Pastor*, (Zondervan, 1996), quoted in 'Netfax 49,' The Leadership Network, 8 July 1996, http://www.leadnet.ord/d1dnetfax49.html

15 Nick Cave, Introduction to Mark's Gospel, *pocket canon*, (Canongate: Edinburgh, 1998), http://www.canongate.co.uk/

16 Tony Benn in 'Leadership into the 21st Century,' *The Times*, London, in Association with the Industrial Society, 9 February 1999.

17 David A. Nadler, *Champions of Change* (Jossey-Bass Publishers, San Fransisco, 1998), quoted in Terence Ryan *The Changing Economy, Information Communication Technology and New Forms of Business Management: What they Could Mean for Education Systems*. Paper for the 21st Century Learning Initiative, April 1998. www.learn.org

18 Paddy Ashdown, quoted in 'Knowing when to bow out,' Eve-Ann Prentice, *The Times*, London, 9 February 1999.

19 Sir Clive Thompson, President of the Confederation of British Industry, quoted in 'A duty to inspire love and harmony,' Susan MacDonald, *The Times*, London, 9 February 1999.

20 George Bullard, website quote, Leadership Network, http://www.leadnet.org

21 Lord Archer of Weston-Super-Mare, 'Set an Example,' in *The Times*, London, 9 February 1999.

22 Sarah, eighteen-year-old ex-member of the Jesus Army, quoted in 'Christian Soldiers,' *Time Magazine*, 27 January 1997.

23 James Robertson, *The Sane Alternative*, 1983.

24 Quoted in Susan MacDonald, 'A duty to inspire love and harmony,' *The Times*, London, 9 February 1999.

25 *Ibid.*

26 Quoted by John Abbot, 21st Century Learning Initiative, seminar, 1997 http://www.21learn.org

27 Loren Mead, *op. cit.*

APPENDIX

Contact address

For comments and questions on the content of *Get a Grip on the Future*, e-mail Gerard Kelly at:

Getagrip@cafe.surfaid.org

Or visit the book's web page at:

http: //www.users.surfaid.org/~cafe/getagrip. htm

Café.net

This is a network of Christians active in the future of Europe. It is a small organisation started by Gerard and Chrissie Kelly to foster innovation and creativity in mission.

Our mission statement is

We will use every method at our disposal to promote, initiate, nurture and support Christian mission in twenty-first-century Europe.

This is implemented in three areas of activity

NETWORK—bringing together Christians with a passion for Europe and a focus on the future. Linking innovative missions projects to one another and to a wider web of prayer.

EXPOSURE—building short-term teams to carry support, encouragement and resources to frontline missions projects in Europe. Café.net trips combine elements of pilgrimage and mission in the *peregrine* ethos, asking participants to 'take something with you—bring something back.'

TRAINING—providing research, resources and training opportunities specific to the challenges of Christian mission in twenty-first-century Europe.

For details contact

Café.net
Chawn Hill Christian Centre
Chawn Hill
Stourbridge
West Midlands
DY9 7JD
UK

e-mail   info@cafe.surfaid.org
web site   http://www.users.surfaid.org/~cafe